Celebrating Irish
SALMON

Ceiliúradh an Bhradáin

dedication

In memory of my parents,
Máirtín Mac Con Iomaire,
the talented ghillie, and Kate,
the wonderful and inspiring
cook. I thank them both for
instilling in me love, passion
and respect for the sea and
the wonders of its bounty.

tiomnú

I gcuimhne ar mo thuismitheoirí,
Máirtín Mac Con Iomaire,
iascaire slaite den scoth, agus
Kate, a mhúscail suim agus grá
na cócaireachta ionam i m'óige.
Mo mhíle buíochas leo beirt
agus 'i líonta Dé go gcastar sinn'.

Celebrating Irish
SALMON

Ceiliúradh an Bhradáin

Máirín Uí Chomáin

Foreword by Ken Whelan

Photography by Walter Pfeiffer

ARTISAN HOUSE EDITIONS

CREATED WITH PASSION

Books of taste
created with passion
in the heart of Connemara

www.artisanhouse.ie

acknowledgements

I would like to thank my publishers, Mary Ruddy and Vincent Murphy of Artisan House Editions, most sincerely for helping me fulfil my dream to publish this book. Not alone did they help me but they encouraged me every day to keep my dream alive. They are as much a part of this book as I am.

We were privileged to have Prof. Ken Whelan, a scholar and expert on salmon, to write the foreword to this book. My publishers and I have netted a great catch in this marine biologist. We thank you so much, Ken. Also a big thanks to Rachel McNicholl for her meticulous editing of my recipes. To food stylist extraordinaire, Tricia Doyle, for her creative presentations of my recipes and to Betty Murphy and Peter Dunne for their well-informed and imaginative beverage notes, thank you.

What do I say about my photographer, Walter Pfeiffer, one of the very best. Walter has come on board once more, as he did in 2004 when he photographed my *Irish Oyster Cuisine* book. This gives me great pride.

Thank you to all the chefs, Michelin stars, Euro-Toques and all others who were so generous in giving their time and expertise to supply a recipe. I greatly appreciate your contributions, which have added enormously to the diversity of recipes in the book.

To my big brother Michael, who helped jog my memory regarding fishing tackle and flies and all the stories of my childhood by the river at Casla. *Míle buíochas, a stór.*

To Máire Ní Thuathail, who sat at my table when the seeds of this book germinated, and was always a great support.

Thank you to Anne and John Commins, who nurtured me and indeed kept me fed from their farm in the next field.

Finally, without the love and understanding of my four grown-up children, I might have caved in. Thank you, Fíona, Ríona, Cormac and Treasa.

Sonas agus rath oraibh go léir.

buíochas

Tá mé thar a bheith buíoch do na foilsitheoirí, Mary Ruddy agus Vincent Murphy, Artisan House Editions, faoina ndíogras agus spreagadh chun an leabhar seo a chur ar an saol. Chabraidh said go mór liom le mo bhrionglóid, agus is linn triúr an leabhar seo.

Is mór an phribhléid domsa agus do na foilsitheoiri Mary agus Vincent gur thoiligh an saineolaí agus scoláire bradán, an Prof. Ken Whelan, réamhrá an leabhair seo a scríobh. Níl do shárú le fáil, Ken. Míle buíochas do Rachel McNicholl faoí chumas agus faoí fheabhas a cuid eagarthóireachta. Do'n bhia dhearathóir suntasach, Tricia Doyle, le na teaspántas cruthaitheach do mo chuid oidis, míle maith agus ar ndóigh mo bhuiochas do Betty Murphy agus Peter Dunne a chuir ar an eólas muid agus a thug samhlaíocht dúinn cén deoch a bheadh feiliúnach do na miasa éagsúla. Bhúr sláinte.

Is é an grianghrafadóir cáiliúil Walter Pfeiffer a thóg na pictiúir de na miasa. Roinn cócairí breátha na tíre a gcuid saothair go fial liom. Chuir na miasa éagsúla seo, agus a gcuid smaointe siúd ar an mbradán, go mór le saibhreas agus substaint an leabhair.

Do mo dheartháir mór Micheál a mhúscail smaointe agus nósa m'óige, agus a thug siar ar bhóithrín na smaointe mé agus ar abhainn Chasla.

Do Mháire Ní Thuathail a shuigh ag bord liom agus síol an leabhair seo á chur.

Do mo ghaolta béal dorais, Anne agus John Commins, a choinnigh cothú liom ón ngarraí, buíochas mór.

Ar ndóigh, ní bheadh croí ar bith ionam chun an leabhar seo a scríobh murach grá mo chlainne, Fíona, Ríona, Cormac agus Treasa.

Gach sonas agus rath oraibh go léir.

contents

introduction salmon – the prince of fish

máirín uí chomáin

My earliest memory is my father's cap. The fact that I wasn't allowed to touch it added to its appeal and mystique. But it was the array of peacock colours I loved: fluorescent pinks and orange, lime and avocado greens, cobalt and aqua blues, silvers, specks of white and Connemara black.

My father's tweed cap was his store room for the various *cuileóga bréige* (flies): Peter Ross, Murrough, Pearly Invicta, Bibio, Sooty Olive. The day, the light, the fish, the time of year and the wind were all factors determining which fly would be used. Máirtin Ridge, my father, was the ghillie on abhainn Chasla (Costello river) for about 30 years. The river was then owned by Bruce Ismay of *Titanic* fame (or infamy).* We imbibed our father's knowledge and conversation about that river and the salmon that swam in it as they made their way upstream to the lakes in Glenicmurrin and Fermoyle after their epic journey at sea.

Our family of ten children and my parents lived in the Bridge House on abhainn Chasla. My mother, Kate, cooked and fed not only her family but also guests who called for lunch and afternoon tea. Wild salmon, trout and eel were the mainstay of our diet during the summer season.

My training in seafood started early and was formalised when I was lucky enough to gain a scholarship to train as a teacher of Home Economics in St Catherine's College, Sion Hill, Co. Dublin. My first teaching job was in 1957 on the Aran Islands, where I was given the task, in addition to teaching second level students, of teaching young fishermen how to cook for themselves during their long fishing trips at sea.

I met my husband-to-be, Patrick (Pakie) Commins, on Aran, so it holds many warm memories for me. Later, in the 1960s, we moved to the US and I got a position in menu planning in the kitchens of Cornell University, where Pakie was studying.

It was while in the US that I witnessed how various ethnic groups treasured their native dishes. For the first time, I appreciated the rich inheritance I had been given. I returned to Dublin in 1966 full of new confidence, energy, love for the sea and all its bounty, and for the Irish kitchen and its creative use of this bounty. I was fortunate that my return coincided with a growing awareness in Ireland of the quality of our produce, spearheaded by Myrtle Allen in Ballymaloe, Co. Cork. I wish to acknowledge and honour Myrtle and her pioneering work. Over the decades, she has been and continues to be an inspiration to me.

I continued to teach, and on Pakie's retirement we moved back to the west of Ireland, setting up home within an oar's length of the Galway shoreline. Sadly, Pakie has now left this world, but he still guides me. It is here, overlooking Galway Bay, with the assistance of Artisan House Editions and the generous contributors, that I am realising my dream book to celebrate the prince of all fish, the wonderful Atlantic salmon.

* J. Bruce Ismay was the chairman of the International Mercantile Marine Company, owners of the *Titanic*. He survived the fateful maiden voyage in 1912. As the ship was sinking he boarded a lifeboat and was subsequently rescued. However, this action led to his vilification in the press for deserting the ship while women and children were still on board. Ismay kept out of the public eye for the remainder of his life and settled with his wife in Costello Lodge, in Connemara, Co. Galway until the 1930s. He died in London in 1937. His reputation never recovered.

| Blue Charm | Connemara Black | Fiery Brown | Lemon Grey | Thunder & Lightning | Jock Scott |

Hand-made salmon flies presented to Brian McNicholl by Noel Huggard of the Butler Arms, former owner of Ashford and Ballynahinch castles. May they fish together in the next life.

Teach an Droichid, Abhainn Chasla, le Charles Lamb RHA

Is é caipín m'athar an pictiúr is daingne i m'aigne. Is é an bac a bhí orm gan dul i ngar dhó a chuidigh leis an mistéir.

Bhí an caipín ildaite cóirithe leis na *cuileóga bréige* ba dheise dath ó oráiste, go gorm, ó ghlas go cobailt, cosúil le gath gréine dáirírc; agus ba é sin a áit stórala dhá úirlisí mealadh bradán. Bhí úsáid na gcinn éagsúla ag brath ar an lá, an solas agus tráth na bliana.

Bhí m'athair, Máirtín Mac Con Iomaire, mar ghiolla nó fear slaite ar abhainn Chasla le blianta siar. Ba le Bruce Ismay an abhainn ag an tráth sin; siúd é an fear ar fhág tragoid an *Titanic* droch shéala ar a shaol.* Shúigh muid isteach eolas agus seanachas ár n-athar faoln abhainn agus na bradáin maorga a thaisteal inti agus iad ag trial ar loch Ghleann Mhic Mhuirinn agus Fhoramaoil.

Thóg Máirtín agus Kate deichniúr clainne i dTeach an Droichid agus chomh maith le beatha a choinéal linne bhíodh mo mháthair ag freastal agus ag beathú stráinséaraí agus cuairteoirí chun na háite. Bradán, liathán agus eascain a bhíodh ar bord againn formhór an t-séisiúr.

Bhí mé sa chistin ó bhí mé beag ach ba í an scoláireacht go Coláiste San Caitríona i gCnoc Síon, áit ar hoileadh mé mar mhúinteoir tís, mo chéad chéim le m'aisling a chur i gcrích. Bhí mo chéad phost mar mhúinteoir tís agam i nGairmscoil Éinne, Cill Rónáin, Árainn sa mbliain 1957. Chomh maith le scoláirí dara leibhéal a

bheith faoi mo chúram, bhí mé freisin ag treorú iascairí óga chun iad féin a choinneáil beathaithe agus iad ag treabhadh na farraige. Is i gCill Rónáin a bhuail mé le Páraic Ó Comáin, go ndéana Dia grásta air, agus é mar phríomhoide agam. Mo bhrón nach bhfuil sé linn a thuilleadh ach tá a chuid ionspioráide liom go cinnte. Chaith muid cúpla bliain ag Ollscoil Chornell sna seacaidí, áit a raibh seisean ag staidéar agus mise ag obair ag pleanáil biachláir do mhic léinn an choláiste.

Siúd é an áit a spreag mé chun níos mó measa agus bróid a bheith agam as ár mbia agus ár dtraidisiúin féin. Thug mé faoi deara an meas a bhí ag na ciníocha éagsúla ar a mbia dúchais féin. Chuir sé ag smaoineamh mé ar an oidhreacht beatha a bhí againn ag baile.

D'fhill mé ar ais sa bhliain 1966 lán le muinín, brí agus grá do'n fharraige agus dá saibhreas. Bhí sé tráthúil thart ar an am céanna go raibh bia na tíre seo ag dul i dtreo níos gairimiúla, agus cuid mhór de seoag tarlú de bharr tionchar Myrtle Allen as Ballymaloe. Ba i a bhí mar cheannródaí bia sa tír agus ba mhaith liom a admháil go raibh Myrtle mar inspioráid agamsa agus go mbeidh go deo. Bean uasal, speisialta.

Cormac Ó Comáin ar Abhainn An Mhuaidh

Anois agus mé ag cur fúm le hais chuan na Gaillimhe, foilsitheoirí breátha agam in Artisan House Editions, agus scothchócairí na tíre ag roinnt a gcuid oideas liom, tá mian mo chroí faigthe agam agus an leabhar seo á fhoilsiú.

* Ba é Bruce Ismay Cathaoirleach an chómhlacht Mercantile Marine Company, úinéirí an *Titanic*. Tharraing sé droch cháil ar féin nuair a tháinic sé slán ó thubaiste uafásach na loinge sin sa bhliain 1912 i gceann de na báid tarrthála, tráth ar bádh líon mór paisinéirí. D'imigh sé as amharc an tsaoil ansin agus chónaí sé féin agus a bhean i Lodge Chasla i gConamara, go dtí na naoí déag triochaidí. Fuair sé bás i Londain sa bhliain 1937 gan a ainm glanta aige.

foreword Ireland's silver treasure
ken whelan

Surprisingly, my first introduction to salmon and salmon fishing had nothing to do with angling. As a young student in the early 1970s, I applied for a summer bursary with the Department of Agriculture and Fisheries and was subsequently dispatched to County Kerry for nine weeks. My home that glorious summer was a Departmental tent and my stipend was the princely sum of £12

Releasing a salmon back into the river

per week. As I took biological samples from the shore-based salmon fisheries in Kenmare, I was privileged to work closely with the local fishermen. Skilled observers of the salmon's every move, they watched with eager intensity the V-shaped

formations of fish as they entered the bay. Watching and praying, the fishermen waited for the first jump of the lead salmon at the apex of the group, which signalled a rush to the boats and a frantic but well-organised scramble to launch the nets ahead of the shoal. This was tough, gruelling and highly skilled work, but despite the physical efforts required to trap their quarry, the salmon was held in the highest esteem. The battle with the salmon was personalised by always referring to a shoal of salmon in the singular as 'a fish', and even when a shoal evaded capture and sneaked under the base of the net, I often heard the fishermen remark, 'Well, that's one for the river.'

I'm fortunate that my career as a salmon biologist has enabled me to work in some of the most remote and beautiful places on earth. From the wilds of the Kola Peninsula in Western Russia to the headwaters of the giant salmon rivers of New Brunswick, I have found among the native peoples this common thread of respect for the wild Atlantic salmon. Here, on the island of Ireland, we are guardians of over 150 distinct stocks of salmon, ranging from the highly productive river systems such as the Moy and the Foyle to the almost inconsequential populations of salmon to be found in the smaller, west coast sea-trout fisheries, such as that of Casla, near Costello in Connemara, where Máirín's father, Máirtín, worked and fished throughout his life. Although these smaller stocks are relatively low in abundance, we now know that they add greatly to the overall biodiversity of the species, and who knows, such tiny, discrete populations may well hold genes which are vital to the very survival of the species in the decades to come.

Ken Whelan and Markus Müller fishing on Carrowmore Lake

T.C. Kingsmill Moore in his iconic angling book *A Man May Fish* describes the waters of the Casla system in intimate, loving detail. Máirtín doubtless knew the great man and may even have ghillied for him, or at the very least shepherded him in his pony and trap to the high lakes at the very top of the Casla system. I'm sure during these times together their conversations turned to the future of their quarry and the hope that generations to come would, as they had, revere, protect and enhance Ireland's silver treasure.

PROF. KEN WHELAN BSC, PHD, FIFM

Anglers fishing the Ridge Pool, River Moy, Ballina

preparation and cooking

Salmon can rightly claim to be the perfect food. It is relatively low in calories, high in protein and contains omega–3 fatty acids. It is easy to cook and can be married with lots of different flavours, as you will see in the following treasure trove of recipes.

preparation methods

Scaling

Removing the scales from the salmon is not a necessity but cooks like to de-scale the fish if the skin is to be eaten or to prevent scales dropping off and spoiling the presentation.

If scaling, it is easier to do before the salmon is gutted.

Wash the fish and lay it on one side. Work near a water source as it is easier to remove scales when fish is wet. To remove scales, go 'against the grain', working from tail to head. Place the sharp edge of the knife against the skin at an angle of about 45°. Using short strokes, scrape the knife edge over the skin, lifting the scales and removing them. When one side is completed, turn and repeat on the other side. You will notice a loss of sheen on the skin after the scales have been removed.

Gutting

Make a cut from the gills to the vent. Entrails should be removed intact by cutting through where they attach to the back of the head. To remove blood in the kidney (the deep red mass that runs along the backbone), slit open with the tip of a knife. Using the back of a spoon, squeeze out the blood by gently sliding the spoon along the backbone. Wash thoroughly under a running cold tap, ensuring there are no traces of blood or guts left in the cavity. If cooking the salmon whole, remove the dorsal fin by cutting along each side and carefully pulling the fin out with pliers.

Skinning

Place the salmon fillets on a board with the tail towards you, flesh side up.

Using a sharp, flat-bladed (not serrated) knife make a small nick backwards through the flesh but not through the skin.

This gives you something to grip. Change the direction of the knife and keep both knife and skin flat on the board.

Work towards the top of the fillet using a saw-like motion. The skin should come away in one piece.

recipe measurements

All the recipes list both metric and imperial measurements. Conversions are approximate and have been rounded up or down.

Follow one set of measurements only, do not mix the two.

Spoon measures

Spoon measurements are level unless otherwise specified.

1 teaspoon = 5 ml
1 dessertspoon = 10 ml
1 tablespoon = 15 ml

The salmon embellished some of our Irish coinage up until 1993.

basic cooking methods

Salmon is a very versatile food and lends itself to many different cooking methods. It also cooks quickly so care should be taken not to over-cook and thus spoil the flavour and texture. Remember, salmon will continue to cook after you remove it from heat.

Once cooked, fish loses its translucent look and will flake easily.

Poaching
This is a suitable method of cooking for most types of fish, including salmon. The salmon may be poached in fish stock, milk or water, with seasonings. Place the fish in the simmering liquid, bring to a steady simmer and poach for 5–8 minutes depending on the thickness of the fish. The liquid may be used as a base for a sauce or soup.

Steaming
This method of cooking is particularly suited to fillets of salmon. Season well before placing in a steamer, and cover tightly. Place over simmering water and cook for 10–15 minutes depending on the size.

Grilling
Grilling is cooking under a radiant heat and is a fast method of cooking, suitable for fillets. Line the grill with foil and brush lightly with oil. Preheat the grill. Use even-sized pieces of salmon when grilling. Oil the fish lightly and turn the fish only once during cooking as it is delicate and may break easily.

Baking
Salmon can be successfully baked in the oven. It may be placed on a bed of vegetables, wrapped in a foil or greaseproof paper parcel or placed in a casserole dish. Preheat the oven to 190 °C / 375 °F / Gas mark 5 and allow 15–25 minutes depending on size of the salmon.

You can also cook at a lower temperature of 140 °C / 275 °F / Gas mark 1, which allows the salmon to cook gently retaining its moist texture. This is a particularly suitable cooking method for a whole salmon. Allow cooking time of 1 hour 10 minutes for 700 g / 1½ lb salmon and 2 hours 30 minutes for a 1.8–2.25 kg / 4–5 lb salmon.

Frying
Frying is probably the most popular method of cooking all fish, including salmon. When possible, fry the salmon with the skin on, even if you remove it before serving.

The subcutaneous fat layer under the skin acts as a heat barrier and helps to alleviate over-cooking problems and retain moisture.

Shallow-frying
Use a mixture of oil and butter when frying and only turn the fish once during cooking.

A ridged pan is a great utensil for frying fish (see p. 12).

Deep-frying
The fish should be coated before frying. Use a suitable container and heat the oil to 190 °C / 375 °F. Test the temperature before starting to cook the fish. After removing from oil, drain the cooked fish very well on absorbent paper.

Stir-frying
This is a very fast method of cooking. Use a wok or deep-frying pan. Food for stir-frying should be cut into thin strips and seasoned before cooking begins. This is a very suitable method of cooking for all firm-fleshed fish.

Microwave cooking
Salmon cooks beautifully in a microwave oven. Use a suitable non-metallic dish and cook even-sized pieces together. Fish is so moist it can be cooked in little or no liquid, so none of the flavour is lost.

When cooking thin fillets turn the tail pieces under to give even thickness. As cooking will continue when fish is removed from the microwave, allow the fish to stand for 2–5 minutes before serving.

Sous vide
'Sous vide' is a method of cooking food sealed in airtight plastic bags in a water bath for a prolonged period at a very precise temperature.
Sous vide is a French term meaning 'under vacuum'.

cooking terms

Reducing

Reducing is a simple technique that delivers an intensely flavoured sauce-like consistency to a liquid by bringing it to a rapid boil and allowing steam to escape from the pan, thereby reducing the original volume. In general the reduction should cling to the back of a spoon. The secret is to ensure you do not put a lid on the pan as this prevents the steam escaping.

Blanching

Blanching is a process where food, usually a vegetable or fruit, is plunged into boiling water, removed after a brief time, 30 seconds to 1 minute usually, and plunged into iced water to halt the cooking process.

cooking equipment

Bain-marie

A bain-marie, also known as a double boiler or water bath, comes in a variety of sizes and types but is basically a smaller container that fits inside a larger outer container that holds the water. It cooks or keeps food warm at an even temperature. You can improvise at home with a large saucepan half filled with water, into which you sit a smaller saucepan. If it's for oven use, sit a smaller dish or dishes into a large casserole dish and fill it with water to below the top of the smaller dish(es).

Ridged pan

A ridged pan is a great utensil in any household. Use a cast-iron pan if you can, as its heavy weight allows it to achieve very high temperatures and give that signature charred flavour. By using the ridged pan you can ensure that your fish or meat does not sit in the juices it releases during cooking. Treat a ridged pan well and it will last a lifetime, performing better and better with age.

smoked salmon

Salmon is smoked by one of two methods: hot smoking or cold smoking.

Generally, the fresh salmon is salted, dried, washed, then air-dried and smoked over wood chippings.

Hot smoking effectively 'cooks' the fish, because it is smoked over heat for six to 12 hours.

Cold smoked fish is first cured or preserved either in dry salt or brine, then smoked at a much lower temperature usually for 24 to 48 hours, but it can be longer.

This is the style that most people associate with 'smoked salmon'.

The actual smoking process varies a great deal, with each smokehouse using its own techniques.

Be aware of the ambiguity of labels: a label that reads 'Irish Smoked Salmon' can mean salmon from any source smoked in Ireland, while 'Smoked Irish Salmon' means salmon sourced in Ireland.

caviar and salmon roe

True caviar is the salted and matured eggs or roe of the female sturgeon, traditionally from the Caspian Sea. The eggs are usually a pearly greyish-black in colour and vary in size. Beluga is the most expensive variety, prized for its soft, extremely large (pea-size) eggs. The oscietra and sevruga caviars are produced from different species of sturgeon. Sturgeon populations in the Caspian Sea are under extreme pressure, with breeding stocks of some species critically low. Consequently, environmentally conscious chefs and consumers have been exploring other types of fish roe as an alternative. Avruga is a caviar substitute made from herring roe. Lumpfish roe and salmon roe are other good and less expensive alternatives.

You can buy caviar in tins or jars. The roe should be firm but soft and moist and never dry. Do not use a metal spoon to serve caviar as it taints the berries. A mother-of-pearl spoon is the preferred implement for caviar.

Caviar perishes quickly so make sure it is kept in the fridge.

beverage notes

betty murphy and peter dunne

The choice of guests, rather than the choice of food and wine, is the secret to a successful dinner party – but getting all three right leads to a memorable occasion.

It is a common misconception that fish is always best accompanied by white wine. This is true for many fish dishes, but as you will see from our suggestions, we also recommend some red wines. Gamay is delightful with chargrilled salmon; a light red burgundy, such as Mercurey, is perfect with poached salmon.

In some of our pairings, Champagne is king, but we also love Prosecco, Fino sherry (great with hot-smoked salmon) or Manzanilla, the queen of sherry aperitifs.

And we do not limit ourselves to the grape. Beautiful organic smoked Irish salmon deserves a special partner: we recommend trying it with a few drops of a Single Pot Still whiskey, such as Green Spot, sprinkled over the serving platter. Other suggestions include sake, an Irish craft beer or cider, and who can go wrong with Guinness or Murphy's served with brown bread and smoked salmon.

The best pairing advice is to serve simple wines with complex food and complex wines with simple food. Ultimately, taste is subjective, but as long as the drink complements and enriches the dish and doesn't distort or overpower, then it's the right choice.

Have fun with pairing: try out something new or encourage your friends to bring a surprise bottle to match the food some evening. We recall an evening in Connemara with Artisan House Editions and friends when we put dishes of smoked salmon, hot-smoked salmon, poached wild salmon and salmon in honey and mustard sauce on the table. We lined up a bottle of Australian Clare Valley Riesling, Hidalgo Fino sherry, Château de Sours rosé from Bordeaux, a Jameson whiskey, a can of Guinness and an array of glasses. We had great fun, differing opinions and a rainbow of tasting and smelling experiences.

Keep experimenting, and take advice from your local wine shop or from the sommelier if you are dining in a restaurant.

Some of our favourite wine accompaniments for salmon

The Chardonnay grape is one of the most versatile in the wine world, ranging from rare Burgundies and classic Chablis to the fruit-filled giant whites of the New World.

Chenin Blanc from the Loire and South Africa, with its mix of mild herb and honey, is ideal for poached salmon and creamy sauces.

Albariño, from Spain, has enough aniseed and liquorice tones to match the ingredients of lightly spiced dishes.

The magic Riesling grape varies in style from the low-alcohol wines of the Mosel region to the strong almond and pear styles of New Zealand. Ideal for the stronger or spicy recipes and smoked fish of any sort.

The aromatic Sauvignon Blanc grape is always a winner with salmon. The choice is wide, from minerally Sancerre, Pouilly-Fumé and Menetou-Salon to the more fruity New Zealand varieties.

The honey and apricot flavours of the Viognier grape can be a good match for a smoked salmon recipe or one containing spices and ginger.

Gewürztraminer is a floral wine with spice and enough body to complement ginger or saffron flavoured dishes as well as smoked salmon.

Gamay, a grape traditionally linked with Beaujolais Villages, produces light, low-tannin reds that go very well with chargrilled salmon.

Gevry-Chambertin, a burgundy with intricate earthy, musty scents, is a great red for wild salmon.

bites & starters

smoked salmon blinis

This recipe is a modification of the classic blini and caviar combination. I use wheat flour rather than the buckwheat that is usually associated with blinis, as I like the lighter consistency. If you are hosting a small gathering for drinks or preparing a sit-down first course, blinis are ideal. Preparation is simple and can be done in advance, but do not complete the presentation until ready to serve or the blinis will become soggy.

serves 4

topping
50 g / 2 oz smoked salmon
15 g / ½ oz black lumpfish caviar
15 g / ½ oz salmon roe
50 g / 2 oz cream cheese
sprig of dill, finely chopped
sprig of dill, for garnish
pinch salt

blinis
110 g / 4 oz white self-raising flour
1 medium egg
4 tablespoons natural yogurt
110 ml / 4 fl oz milk
sunflower oil, for frying

Mix flour with salt, yogurt, egg and milk in a bowl and whisk to a smooth thick batter.

Heat a heavy pan, oil lightly and drop spoonfuls of mixture into it.

Cook until blinis start to bubble, turn them over, and cook the other side until golden.

Mix the chopped dill with the cream cheese.

To serve, place a spoonful of cream cheese with dill on all of the blinis.

Then top half of them with smoked salmon garnished with black caviar, the other half with salmon roe garnished with dill.

This recipe screams for a Manzanilla sherry, Lustau or La Guita, Jerez, Spain. From the Palomino grape but with a hint of salt on the finish. Or, if the occasion demands it, a pink Champagne from Montaudon, Marguet, Veuve Cliquot or Bollinger.

rustic potted salmon

This is an incredibly easily prepared dish that tastes wonderful, looks very inviting and allows you to taste and enjoy the differing textures of the cooked and smoked salmon.

serves 6

450 g / 1 lb cooked fresh salmon, finely flaked
225 g / 8 oz smoked salmon, finely chopped
2 teaspoons crème fraiche
4 teaspoons creamed horseradish
2 lemons, juice only
2 teaspoons chives, roughly chopped
salt and pepper

By hand, fold all the ingredients together except salt and pepper.

Ensure you keep the texture rough. Taste and season as required.

Cover and chill for at least 2 hours.

Serve with toasted sourdough bread.

Verdejo, Tortora, Spain. This has all the citrus flavours and mineral complexities required to compete with the horseradish component of this rustic pâté.

smoked salmon pâté with cucumber salad

serves 4

225 g / 8 oz smoked salmon
2 teaspoons horseradish, ready prepared
1 lemon, zest and juice
50 g / 2 oz soft cheese
pinch black pepper

cucumber salad

225 g / 8 oz finely sliced cucumber, de-seeded
1 tablespoon dill, chopped
1 tablespoon caster sugar
1 tablespoon white wine vinegar

Use a hand-held blender to mix together the smoked salmon, horseradish, lemon zest and juice, soft cheese and pinch black pepper. Chill until serving.

Mix the caster sugar and vinegar together until the sugar dissolves. Pour over the cucumber slices, sprinkle chopped dill on top. Chill until serving.

Slice the pâté and serve on salad leaves or Melba toast (see p. 134) with cucumber salad to accompany.

Vinho Verde, Espigueiro, Muros Antigos, Portugal. Soft pear and apple fruits are gentle and light for the delicate pâté and sweetish cucumber. A light spritz on the palate leaves you ready for more.

smoked salmon and crab ramekins

serves 4

110 g / 4 oz smoked salmon, cubed
110 g / 4 oz cooked white crab meat
1 egg, whisked
pinch cayenne pepper
pinch grated nutmeg
1 tablespoon chopped chives
110 ml / ¼ pint cream, whipped

Preheat the oven to 190 °C / 375 °F / Gas mark 5.

Mix together the smoked salmon, crab meat, egg, cream, chives, nutmeg and cayenne pepper.

Do not add salt to this recipe as the smoked salmon contains enough saltiness.

Butter four medium-sized ramekin dishes and fill with the mix. Place in a bain-marie (see p. 12) half filled with boiling water and bake for almost 30 minutes until firm.

Serve in ramekin dishes with slices of toasted ciabatta.

Chablis, 'Le Finage', La Chablisienne, Burgundy, France. Mango and peach fruits with touches of stony mineral. This very good, widely available Chablis will easily take on and enhance the crab, salmon and nutmeg.

smoked salmon salad with golden croutons

serves 4

225 g / 8 oz hot-smoked salmon, cut in chunks
3 thick white bread slices, cubed
3 handfuls mixed salad leaves
2–3 tablespoons Caesar salad dressing (see p. 134)
olive or rapeseed oil, for baking

Preheat the oven to 200 °C / 400 °F / Gas mark 6.

Toss the bread cubes in rapeseed or olive oil. Spread evenly on a baking tray and bake until golden, about 15–20 minutes.

Place salad leaves, hot-smoked salmon and croutons in a large salad bowl, drizzle with Caesar dressing and toss well to mix.

Margaret River White, Cullen, Australia. Semillon, plus small amounts of Chardonnay, Chenin Blanc and Verdelho make up this wonderful wine. Attractive perfumed floral and citrus fruits with an underlying minerality will combine beautifully with the salmon and dressing.

salmon tartare passion

Try this exotic, light and easy-to-prepare dish, ideal for St Valentine's evening or any romantic occasion.

serves 2

110 g / 4 oz wild salmon fillet, skinned
2 passion fruit
¼ red chilli pepper, de-seeded and finely diced
4 coriander leaves, finely chopped
1 lime, zest and juice
sea salt
edible flowers to garnish (borage, chive or wild garlic flowers)

Cut the passion fruit in half and scoop out the flesh, setting it aside in a bowl.

Wash the passion fruit skins and dry with kitchen towel. Set aside for later assembly.

Finely chop the chilli pepper and the mint leaves.

To make the salmon tartare, dice the salmon into 5 mm / ¼ inch cubes. Place in a bowl and sprinkle with lime zest and juice, chilli pepper and coriander. Add two tablespoons of passion fruit flesh to the bowl. Mix well and season with sea salt.

Refrigerate for a minimum of 2 hours to allow the salmon to marinate.

Place the four passion fruit shells on one plate. Fill with the salmon tartare and garnish with edible flowers.

Chardonnay / Pinot Meunier, Roederer Champagne Brut Premier, Louis Roederer, Reims, France. If you like your bubbles smooth and sophisticated, you cannot go wrong with the pears and herbs in this classy one. Perfect for an intimate occasion.

salmon soufflé

serves 4

225 g / 8 oz cooked or hot-smoked salmon, flaked
50 g / 2 oz Parmesan cheese, grated
3 eggs, separated
200 ml / 7 fl oz béchamel sauce (see p. 135)
salt and freshly ground black pepper
butter, for greasing

Preheat the oven to 180 °C / 350 °F / Gas mark 4.
Grease four individual soufflé or ramekin dishes with butter and a dusting of the grated Parmesan cheese.

Whisk the egg yolks into the hot béchamel sauce, off the heat. Add the remaining cheese and season with salt and pepper.

In a very clean bowl, whisk the egg whites with a pinch of salt until stiff. Add the salmon and a little of the egg white to the cheese mixture and mix well. Very gently fold in the remaining egg whites. Divide the soufflé mixture between the four dishes and bake for about 15 minutes until firm and brown on top.

Serve straight from the oven with fingers of buttered toast.

Semillon, Château Garriga, Bordeaux, France. Whites from this region are often overlooked. Soft citrus fruits will not spoil the pleasant sensation of the melt-in-the-mouth soufflé.

salmon tartare in fennel shell

serves 4

225 g / 8 oz wild salmon fillet,
cut in 1 cm / ½ inch cubes
2 fennel bulbs with stem
½ lemon, juice
1 passion fruit, flesh only
8 mint leaves, finely chopped
1 lime, zest and juice
1 teaspoon olive oil
sea salt
black pepper, freshly ground
4 chive or wild garlic flowers

Clean the fennel bulbs, leaving a finger-length of stem on each. Cut off and reserve four intact outer leaves to make shells or cups for the salmon tartare. Place these leaves in a bowl of water containing ice cubes and the lemon juice until required

Dice the remainder of one of the fennel bulbs finely.

In a bowl, gently mix the salmon cubes and diced fennel with the passion fruit flesh, mint leaves, lime zest and juice and 1 tablespoon of olive oil. Season with salt and pepper. Chill until ready to use.

Remove the fennel leaves from water and dry well. Place a leaf on each of four plates and fill the shell with the salmon tartare. Top with chive or wild garlic flower. Serve immediately.

Pinot Blanc (organic), 'Les Avoines', Domaine Jean Fournier, Marsannay, Burgundy. The very dry nose leads on to green fruit and citrus flavours. Good salmon deserves good wine, and this one will marry well with the fish and the liquorice flavours of fennel.

smoked salmon in potato skins

serves 4–8

175 g / 6 oz smoked salmon, cut
or torn into small pieces
4 large potatoes
150 ml / ¼ pint soured cream
bunch chives, chopped
25 g / 1 oz butter, melted
25 g / 1 oz smoked salmon strips,
for garnish

Preheat the oven to 200 °C / 400 °F / Gas mark 6.

Wash the potatoes and dry well, prick with a fork. Place in oven and bake for about 40–50 minutes.
When cooked, cool a little, then cut into quarters and remove most of the potato flesh, leaving a little to cover the skins.

Brush the inside of the skin with melted butter, return to the oven until crisp and golden. Leave to cool.

Mix the soured cream with the chives and the smoked salmon.
Spoon the salmon-and-cream mix into the cooled potato skins just before serving. Garnish with strips of smoked salmon.

Use the leftover potato flesh to make colcannon cakes (see p. 69).

Guinness, Murphy's or a bubbly of choice would serve to down these delicious salmon skins. If you are feeling really adventurous, pour a smidgen of Single Pot Still Irish whiskey over the filled skins and allow them to absorb the heavenly flavours of spices with orchard fruits and barley on a background of toasted oak.

salmon tempura with tartare sauce dip

serves 2

225 g / 8 oz salmon fillet, skinned
50 g / 2 oz plain flour
50 g / 2 oz cornflour
150 ml / ¼ pint ice-cold soda water
(use an unopened bottle)
1 egg white, whisked
sunflower oil, for deep-frying
salt
black pepper, freshly ground

tartare sauce
2 tablespoons mayonnaise
(see p 134)
2 tablespoons crème fraiche
½ teaspoon chives, finely chopped
½ teaspoon fresh tarragon
2 teaspoons capers
1 small gherkin, chopped
¼ teaspoon mustard
1 tablespoon wine vinegar

Mix all the sauce ingredients together, cover and refrigerate for at least 30 minutes before serving.

Sieve the flour, cornflour, salt and pepper into a bowl, fold in egg white and soda water and whisk to make a smooth batter.

Cut the salmon into finger-sized pieces.

Heat the sunflower oil until sizzling.

Dip the strips of salmon in the batter and deep-fry until golden.

Drain on kitchen paper and serve hot with tartare sauce dip.

Sauvignon Blanc / Semillon, Château la Brie, Bergerac, France. Good value for a clean herby white with a little creamy, soft aftertaste, thanks to the 10% Semillon. It will soak into the tempura and salmon. Unless you are tempted to have a Guinness or beer!

hot-smoked salmon potato salad

serves 4

225 g / 8 oz hot-smoked salmon, flaked
450 g / 1 lb baby new potatoes
2–3 spring onions, chopped
3–4 tablespoons yogurt
2 handfuls baby salad leaves or watercress
dill to garnish

Cook the potatoes, halve and keep warm.

Toss the warm potatoes and spring onions in the yogurt and fold in the flaked salmon.

Place this mix on top of fresh salad leaves or watercress and garnish with dill.

Try something different: Verdicchio, 'Vigna di Gino', San Lorenzo, Marche, Italy. This creamy, nutty wine has a wonderful fullness on the palate, quite complex but excellent with salad.

wild Delphi salmon tartare

This recipe is a very fresh and simple starter. At Delphi Lodge we have the good fortune to be able to use wild salmon freshly caught on the estate by our anglers.

serves 4

250 g / 9 oz fresh salmon fillet, skinned and pin-boned

marinade
1 tablespoon fresh dill, chopped
1 tablespoon fresh coriander, chopped
1 tablespoon fresh mint, chopped
½ lemon, juice
2 tablespoons extra virgin olive oil
1 pinch salt
1 pinch chilli powder
1 teaspoon balsamic vinegar
4 drops Tabasco

Cut the salmon into small cubes.

Mix all the marinade ingredients in a bowl and stir with a wooden spoon until well combined. Taste and add seasoning if necessary.

Add the salmon cubes to the marinade ensuring it is well covered.

Cover the bowl with cling film and refrigerate for at least 3 hours to allow the flavour of the herbs to infuse the salmon. Remove from the fridge at least 30 minutes before serving to bring salmon back up to room temperature.

Serve the tartare with lettuce tossed in olive oil and lemon juice dressing, and freshly baked brown bread (see p. 137), slightly toasted.

Fino Sherry, Hidalgo, Jerez, Spain. The sharp, dry flavour of this aperitif will be a perfect partner for the salmon tartare. At only 15% proof, you can afford a generous glass for everyone!

smoked salmon and potato bouchées

serves 4

225 g / 8 oz smoked salmon
2–4 tablespoons crème fraiche
250 g / 9 oz potatoes, cooked and mashed
50 g / 2 oz flour
25 g / 1 oz butter, melted
pinch salt
butter and oil, for frying

Mix the mashed potatoes, flour, butter and salt in a bowl.

Turn out on a floured board, divide in two and roll out each piece in a circle.

Using a tiny scone cutter, stamp out little potato cakes.

Fry on hot pan in mix of butter and oil, until golden on both sides.

Serve on a platter with a dollop of crème fraiche and a strip of smoked salmon on top of each one.

Cava Brut, Freixenet Cordon Negro, Penedès, Spain, will complement these delicious mouthfuls.

smoked salmon vichyssoise

The creation of this classic cold leek and potato cream soup is credited to French chef Louis Felix Diat during his tenure at the Ritz–Carlton hotel in New York in the early part of the twentieth century. I enjoyed adding the salty, smoky flavour of Irish smoked salmon. Vichyssoise is traditionally served cold, as in this recipe, but can be served hot.

serves 8

110 g / 4 oz smoked salmon, chopped
4 leeks, cleaned and sliced (white part only)
1 onion, finely chopped
50 g / 2 oz butter
1 litre / 1¾ pint chicken stock or white stock
2 medium potatoes, finely cubed
salt and ground white pepper
200 ml / 7 fl oz cream
25 g / 1 oz salmon roe
chives, finely chopped

In a heavy-based saucepan, lightly sauté the leeks and onion in the melted butter until tender.
Add the stock and potatoes, simmer until potatoes are cooked and leave aside to cool fully.
Add in the smoked salmon and blend until it is very smooth in texture.
Stir in the cream and check for seasoning.
Chill thoroughly for at least 2–3 hours.
Serve the chilled soup in demitasses or small cups, topped with salmon roe and chive garnish.

Tio Pepe or Mitchell's University Fino sherry, Jerez, Spain. Nowadays much lighter at 15% and made from the Palomino grape. A traditional partner to soup (in it or with it). It must be drunk fresh and preferably from a chilled half-bottle.

warm smoked salmon starter

serves 4

450 g / 1 lb smoked salmon, thinly sliced
olive oil
lemon juice
salt and pepper

sauce
6 tablespoons fish stock (see p. 136)
6 tablespoons vermouth
2 tablespoons dry white wine
1 shallot, finely chopped
300 ml / ½ pint cream
25 ml / 1 fl oz medium cream sherry
50 g / 2 oz leek, finely chopped (white part only)
25 g / 1 oz butter
chives, finely chopped

Preheat oven to 200 °C / 400 °F / Gas mark 6.
Get four oven-proof starter plates and fan the salmon slices equally on each.
Lightly brush with olive oil and lemon juice and season with salt and pepper.

In a saucepan boil the fish stock, chopped shallot, wine and vermouth until reduced (see p. 12) to about 25 ml / 1 fl oz.
Strain into a clean saucepan, add the cream, sherry and leek, and heat to reduce to a coating consistency.
Whisk the butter into this sauce and season to taste.
Spoon the sauce over the salmon on the plates, place in the heated oven and bake for 2–3 minutes depending on thickness of fish.

Serve hot, garnished with the chives.

Pinot Gris, Sipp Mack, Alsace, France. This full-bodied white has a touch of spice which will complement the creamy alcohol components of the dish.

smoked salmon gazpacho

The word 'gazpacho' is widely believed to have come from the Arabic, meaning 'soaked bread'. It is now associated with the Andalusian area of Spain, where stale bread, garlic, tomatoes, olive oil, salt and vinegar are the main ingredients for the dish. It is traditionally served cold. There are many modern versions of gazpacho, and I am adding mine, featuring Irish smoked salmon. I am giving two methods; the second one is fun and allows guests to add what they like to the basic gazpacho. I recommend topping it off with some golden croutons (see p. 21).

serves 4

110 g / 4 oz smoked salmon, finely cubed
½ small cucumber, peeled, de-seeded and finely cubed
1 ripe avocado, diced small
1 large ripe tomato, diced small
½ orange or red pepper, de-seeded and diced small
2 scallions, white part only, finely chopped
1 clove garlic, finely crushed
600 ml / 1 pint tomato juice
1 tablespoon tomato purée
1 teaspoon Tabasco
1 lime, juice only
3–4 tablespoons vodka (optional)
celery salt
black pepper, freshly ground

garnish
25 g / 1 oz smoked salmon strips
coriander oil (see p. 136)
coriander leaves

Method 1
Excluding the garnish, combine the smoked salmon cubes, the vegetables and the liquids in a blender and liquidise.

Season to taste but be conservative with the celery salt, as the smoked salmon will bring a salty flavour to the soup.

Pour into a jug, add a few ice cubes, cover with cling film and refrigerate for at least 1 hour.

When you are ready to serve, remove gazpacho from the fridge and stir. Ladle the soup into chilled bowls or glasses.

Divide the salmon strips between each and drizzle the coriander oil over each serving.

Garnish with a sprig of coriander.

Method 2
Mix together the tomato juice, tomato purée, lime juice, Tabasco, vodka (if using), crushed garlic and seasoning. Stir well and refrigerate for an hour.

Using six small dishes, place the cubes of salmon, cucumber, avocado, tomato peppers and scallions in separate dishes. Pour the coriander oil into a jug.

Put a cube of ice into each of four chilled cocktail glasses and pour gazpacho mix into each.

Place the six small dishes and coriander oil jug in the centre of the table so guests can help themselves.

For a summer garden setting, try the top-class Merlot / Cabernet Franc, Château de Sours rosé, Bordeaux, France. A deep-coloured rosé with strawberry notes and a lingering finish should be pure heaven with the strong flavours of this soup.

ginger guacamole with wild smoked salmon

This recipe allows a precious and expensive food to go further. Ginger is always good with wild salmon, better than acid lemon juice, which I think ruins the taste of real wild smoked salmon. We like slices served at room temperature – very important – to allow all the flavours develop and for the oils to start to flow. Treat it like cheese, please! The process we use at Woodcock Smokery conserves the fish and gives it a long shelf-life. This conservation process would have been developed by our ancestors to utilise the abundance of fish available and preserve some for use throughout the year.

serves 4

110 g / 4 oz Woodcock Smokery
wild smoked salmon, thinly sliced

guacamole
1 large ripe avocado
½ lime, juice
1 shallot, very finely chopped
1 tomato, skinned, de-seeded,
finely chopped
1 clove garlic, crushed and finely
chopped
½ fresh red chilli, de-seeded and
finely chopped
8 cm / 3 inch piece
fresh ginger

Cut avocado in two and remove stone.
Spoon flesh out into a bowl and mash with fork, add lime juice and mix well.
Add all other guacamole ingredients and mix well.

Remove the salmon from the fridge at least 30 minutes before serving.
Arrange sliced wild smoked salmon on four starter plates with a serving of guacamole on the side.

Viognier, Jean-Luc Colombo, La Violette, Vin de Pays d'Oc, France. Interesting wines and good value abound in the Languedoc-Roussillon area. The low acidity, with honeysuckle and apricot flavours, will complement the ginger and creamy texture of the guacamole.

smoked salmon and prawn dip

Try this quick dip, great for a pre-dinner snack. I like to place the dip in a serving dish and surround it with fresh raw vegetables, washed and prepared as sticks or florets. Celery, carrots, cauliflower, broccoli, French beans and radishes all work well as finger food with this dip.

serves 4–6

225 g / 8 oz smoked salmon
50 g / 2 oz cooked prawns,
de-shelled and de-veined
75 g / 3 oz low-fat cream cheese
25 g / 1 oz butter
150 ml / ¼ pint cream
juice of ½ lemon
black pepper, freshly ground

Place all the ingredients except the prawns into a blender and blend until smooth.

Add the prawns and blend for a few seconds only so the prawns remain chunky.

Serve in a bowl surrounded by crunchy vegetables.

Sauvignon Blanc, Pouilly-Fumé, Raimbault-Pineau, Loire, France. Firm crispness and acidity are called for given the dairy ingredients. This wine has both, as well as a delicious mineral streak to finish.

whiskey-marinated salmon with pickled cucumber and dill cream

This recipe is based on the traditional Scandanavian gravlax. I have substituted the Scandinavian preferred spirit, vodka, with whiskey to add an Irish twist, but many spirits are suitable; for example, Calvados adds a lovely apple flavour to the dish. It is a versatile dish making the perfect starter when served with pickled cucumber and dill cream. It also makes a delicious main course when cooked with a creamy tagliatelle sauce.

serves 8–10

600 g / 1 lb 5 oz salmon fillet, with skin, pin-boned
2 tablespoons sea salt
1 tablespoon caster sugar
1 teaspoon black pepper, crushed
1 cooked beetroot, grated
25 ml / 1 fl oz Irish whiskey
2 star anise
1 lime
5 juniper berries

dill cream
225 ml / 8 fl oz cream, whipped
2½ tablespoons dill, chopped
salt and pepper, to taste

pickled cucumber
225 ml / 8 fl oz white wine vinegar
125 g/ 4 oz caster sugar
1 cucumber, peeled, finely sliced

Salmon
Mix together in a bowl the salt, sugar, pepper, grated beetroot and chopped dill.
Place the salmon skin down in a deep dish and cover in the salt mixture.
Cut the lime into quarters and squeeze on to salmon, pour the whiskey over the salmon, sprinkle the juniper berries and star anise on to the dish. Cover the dish and allow to rest in the fridge for 24 hours. Use within 5 days or freeze and use within one month.

Pickled cucumber
Add the vinegar to the caster sugar and bring to the boil, lower heat and stir until the sugar has dissolved, allow to cool and pour over the cucumber. Soak cucumber in mixture for one hour. Remove the cucumber from the mixture and place in a serving bowl.

Dill cream
Stir the chopped dill into the whipped cream, add salt and pepper to taste.

To serve, remove the salmon from the fridge at least 30 minutes before serving. Scrape the salt coating off the salmon. Finely slice the salmon. Place the salmon slices on a serving plate. Put the dill cream and cucumber pickle in separate serving bowls.

Sauvignon Blanc, 'Comte Lafond' Sancerre, France. Four words mean a heavenly partner to this Irish gravlax: floral, fruity, flint and chalk.

Connemara Smokehouse wild salmon tartare with Goatsbridge trout caviar, white chocolate and toasted pistachios

The excitement of getting the first wild salmon of the season never diminishes. Looking back on my time as a trainee chef in Rosleague Manor in Connemara, I can now fully appreciate the experience and knowledge I gained from observing the way Paddy Foyle treated the fish and the fishermen when they came into his kitchen. Paddy knew that the season was short and fishing was hard work, and he appreciated the quality of freshly caught wild salmon. I carry this with me in my own restaurant and acknowledge the work of fishermen and all artisan producers in bringing us their wonderful produce.

serves 4

225 g / 8 oz Connemara
Smokehouse smoked wild salmon, diced

1½ teaspoons chives, finely chopped

175 g / 6 oz white chocolate
(Valrhona is our favourite)

1 dessertspoon milk

2 egg whites

1 tablespoon lemon juice

225 ml / 8 fl oz double cream

25 g / 1 oz Goatsbridge trout caviar

2 tablespoons olive oil

3 tablespoons pistachio nuts, de-shelled and coarsely crushed

1 teaspoon butter, melted

Add the chocolate to the milk, melt over a low heat and set aside.

Whip egg whites together with lemon juice until soft peaks form.
Whip cream to soft peaks.
Fold egg whites and cream into chocolate mixture and chill for 6 hours.

Preheat the oven to 160 °C / 325 °F / Gas mark 3.

Coat the pistachio nuts in butter and roast in the oven for 10 minutes.

Toss diced salmon with finely chopped chives and olive oil. Chill until ready to serve.
Fill shot glasses in alternate layers with the salmon, white chocolate and pistachios.

Garnish with trout caviar. Serve with toast.

Albariño Bodegas Fillaboa, Rias Baixas, Galicia, Spain. Pineapple and apple notes with a fresh, salty nose will add to this delicate creation.

Foodwriter **Prannie Rhatigan** **Author of** *Irish Seaweed Kitchen* *Co. Sligo* prannie.com

salmon sushi with duileasc crisps

Sushi is really fun to make. Children in particular love to roll their own dinner. Keep wasabi out of their reach as it is very hot. You may also need to keep the duileasc crisps out of their way as they are so delicious there will be none left for the adults!

serves 5

sushi filling

2 organic salmon steaks,
200 g / 7 oz each, with skin,
pin-boned,
1 large carrot, grated
or
asparagus tips, if in season,
briefly steamed

rice

400 g / 14 oz sushi rice or
organic brown rice
450 ml / 16 fl oz cold water,
plenty of cold water for washing
and soaking rice
piece of kombu seaweed,
10 cm / 4 inches long
dash of mirin (optional)

rice dressing

3 dessertspoons lemon juice
3 dessertspoons mirin
generous pinch salt or mixed
seaweeds
1 scant teaspoon dark
brown sugar

5 nori sheets
5 tablespoons homemade
mayonnaise (see p. 134) or
best-quality shop-bought
1–2 teaspoons wasabi, it is hot
so be careful. Use more if you
are used to it.
pickled ginger
soy sauce or tamari

duileasc crisps

25 g / 1 oz dried duileasc
(also known as dulse or dillisk)

equipment

sushi mat or folded tea towel

Duileasc crisps

Using a scissors, cut dried duileasc into 1 inch pieces and dampen very lightly with water. Place on a pan with a little butter and cook over moderate heat for approximately 30 minutes until crisp. Watch them as they can burn easily. Or place in a very low oven for a few hours until crisp.

Sear the salmon by placing it, skin side down, for 1 minute on a lightly oiled pan over high heat and cooking for 2 minutes. Turn the salmon, place a tightly fitting lid on pan, remove from the heat and leave to continue cooking in the pan for at least 10 minutes.

Wash the rice thoroughly until it runs clear and leave it to soak in cold water for 15 minutes. Drain and cook the rice in a saucepan with a tight fitting lid using the 2 cups water, the piece of kombu and dash of mirin, if using. Tip the cooked rice into a large dish and add the dressing, working it through the rice with a wooden spoon until it has cooled.

Sushi rolls

Add the wasabi to the mayonnaise and mix well. Place a nori sheet, shiny side down, on the mat and, using approximately one-fifth of the rice, press it into the nori sheet leaving 1 inch clear at the top. Using one-fifth of the salmon and chosen vegetable, place them from left to right in a line around the lower third of the sheet. Smear on the mayonnaise with wasabi. Using the mat, roll up the sheet like a swiss roll, encasing all the filling very tightly. Squeeze to firm up the roll. Repeat the process for the other sheets. Place rolls on a chopping board and using a very sharp knife slice each roll into 8 pieces. Arrange on a serving plate and serve with extra wasabi, pickled ginger and soy sauce or tamari. Scatter with duileasc crisps.

Sparkling wine, traditional method, Rotari 'Talento' Brut, Trentino, Italy. The dry fragrant flavour, elegant and complex, will ensure enjoyment with this 'Irish' sushi.

cured salmon, fennel panna cotta, pickled mooli, apple, radish and fennel crisp

This is a recipe for a popular amuse-bouche we serve in the Lady Helen Restaurant. It is a light dish with a refreshing flavour which makes a nice start to a meal.

serves 30

cured salmon
½ side of salmon, 400 g / 14 oz with skin, pin-boned

cure
zest of 6 oranges
250 g / 9 oz Maldon sea salt
250 g / 9 oz caster sugar
8 black peppercorns, crushed
6 juniper berries, crushed
2 sprigs thyme leaves, picked

fennel panna cotta
3 heads fennel, finely sliced
50 g / 2 oz potato, diced
2 tablespoons olive oil
1 litre / 1¾ pints water
150 g / 5 oz samphire
50 g / 2 oz spinach leaves, washed
110 ml / 4 fl oz Pernod
1–2 silver leaves gelatin
pepper
2 litres / 3½ pints water

pickled white mooli
250 ml / 9 fl oz white wine vinegar
200 g / 7 oz brown sugar
4 star anise
1 teaspoon mustard seeds
1 teaspoon coriander seeds
1 cinnamon stick
1 white mooli, cut into small balls using a parisienne cutter or melon baller

fennel crisps
¼ loaf sourdough, sliced very thinly
1 teaspoon fennel pollen
olive oil
salt

Trim the side of the salmon. Mix all the cure ingredients together. In a deep tray place a layer of the mixture and then place the salmon skin down. Spread the remaining mixture over the salmon flesh ensuring it is is fully covered. Leave for two days to cure in the refrigerator, and then remove and rinse off any remaining cure. Pat dry and place into fridge.

Fennel panna cotta
The cooking method for the fennel panna cotta calls for a cartouche. A cartouche is basically a type of paper lid which reduces evaporation. Take a square piece of parchment or greaseproof paper, fold in half, and in half again. Hold the tip of the cartouche to the centre of the pan, tear off any paper that extends over the edge, open out to a circle.

Put 2 tablespoons olive oil in a saucepan on a medium high heat and add the fennel slices and diced potatoes. Add 1 litre of water and cover the saucepan with a cartouche. Simultaneously, in another pot, bring 2 litres of water to the boil and add in samphire, cook for 1–2 minutes.

When potatoes and fennel are fully cooked, mix with the cooked samphire and blitz for 6 minutes at high speed in a food processor. Add spinach to the mix and blitz at a lower speed for a further 3 minutes. Strain the purée through a fine sieve, retain in a bowl placed in a larger bowl of ice cubes to keep the bright green colour. Taste and season as needed; samphire is salty so the mixture may require very little or no salt. Whisk in Pernod.

Weigh the panna cotta and for every 200 ml / 7 fl oz use 1 leaf of gelatin. Soak the gelatin in water for 15–20 minutes. Squeeze to remove excess water and add to the purée. Select suitable glasses, lay a generous tablespoon of panna cotta in each glass. Leave to set in the refrigerator for 2–3 hours.

Pickled white mooli
The mooli radish, also known as daikon, is a giant snow-white radish with a mild flavour that can be purchased in Asian supermarkets and speciality outlets.

Bring all ingredients, except the mooli, to a simmer. After 4–5 minutes, remove from the heat and leave to one side to cool. Once fully cooled pour over the mooli and leave for 5–6 hours to infuse.

Fennel crisps
Preheat the oven to 100 °C / 212 °F / Gas mark ¼.

Place the sourdough slices on a flat tray, lightly brush with the olive oil, and sprinkle with fennel pollen and salt to taste. Place in oven until bread is crisp. Remove and leave to cool.

Photography Cormac Rowe

mustard aioli

¼ clove garlic, crushed

1 tablespoon Dijon mustard

2 egg yolks

400 ml / 14 fl oz white wine
vinegar

400 ml / 14 fl oz olive oil

50 ml / 2 fl oz water

salted cucumber

½ cucumber, peeled and
de-seeded

1 teaspoon Maldon sea salt

garnish

5 red breakfast radishes

1 apple

60 leaves red vein sorrel, washed

60 leaves red mustard cress,
washed

Mustard aioli

Place garlic, mustard, egg yolk in a bowl and using a hand blender, blend on medium speed. Add the vinegar and continue to blend until fully incorporated. Slowly add olive oil and continue to blend until the mixture thickens. If it becomes too thick, add a little water. Season to taste and place in refrigerator until needed.

Salted cucumber

Dice the cucumber very finely and lighty season with the sea salt. Leave for 1 hour to infuse. Before serving, strain excess liquid from the cucumber.

Assembly

Remove the cured salmon from the refrigerator at least 30 minutes before serving, and the panna cotta glasses about 15 minutes prior to serving, to allow them come to room temperature.

Cut the salmon into small cubes. Cut the red breakfast radishes in half, and then slice very finely. Place in ice water until serving. Cut the apple into little thin strips and place in iced water with a squeeze of lemon juice. This can be done up to 30 mins before serving.

To serve, place a few dots of mustard aioli on top of the panna cotta. Add salmon cubes, mooli balls, salted cucumber dice, red radish and apple slices, fennel crisps and sorrel and mustard cress leaves.

Muscat, Domaine Rolly-Gassman, Alsace, France. Dry, with peach and apricot perfume, this is the original 'apéro' which never disappoints.

wild salmon sashimi with melon and pomegranate

Pomegranates are among the most antioxidant-rich fruit in the world. They are very good for the heart and also increase your levels of serotonin (happy hormones). Besides, the red seeds look beautiful.

serves 4

225 g / 8 oz wild salmon fillet, skinned
2 cantaloupe melons
1 pomegranate
12 pea shoots
6 edible flowers (e.g. borage, chive or wild garlic, depending on season)
wasabi (or hot horseradish)

Cut the melons into 12 delicate finger-size rectangles. Cut the raw salmon into similar sized pieces.

Using four rectangular plates, place three melon fingers on each plate and top with salmon fingers.

Arrange three pomegranate seeds on each salmon finger and arrange pea shoots and flowers between the fingers.

Place a teaspoon of wasabi on the side.

Try a sake such as Hoyo 'Genji' Sake, full of white flowers, peaches and apricots. A Riesling or a craft beer would also work well.

38

wild salmon ballotine with beet and pomegranate gel, green asparagus and fried Chinese black fungus

This dish may look complicated but is in fact pretty simple and can make an interesting starter. The salmon is more warmed than cooked and this will protect the delicate oils that are so important to wild fish.

serves 1

salmon
90 g / 3½ oz wild salmon or
good organic salmon, de-scaled
and pin-boned
sea salt
olive oil

stock syrup
150 g / 5 oz sugar
150 ml / 5 fl oz water

pomegranate and beet gel
This quantity makes 3 cups but
you can retain any that is not
used and it makes a great
accompaniment to cold meats
as well as fish.
225 ml / 8 fl oz stock syrup
1½ tablespoon agar-agar
225 ml / 8 fl oz beetroot juice
125 ml / 4 fl oz lemon juice
25 ml / 1 oz pomegranate
molasses

vegetable garnish
50 g / 2 oz dried Chinese
black fungus
½ teaspoon butter
sunflower oil, for frying
2 asparagus spears with
ends trimmed, halved lengthways
1 tablespoon fresh pomegranate
seeds
1 thin slice of raw beetroot
edible flowers such as borage or
nasturtiums

Carefully remove the skin from the salmon. Slice the flesh into cubes (about 2.5 cm x 2.5cm / 1 inch x 1 inch). Now wrap the skin around the meat to form a neat cylinder. Brush the skin with olive oil and season with sea salt, then wrap in a little cling film to form the ballotine. Any trimmings of the salmon can be cut into neat cubes, brushed with olive oil and again wrapped tightly in cling film.

Stock syrup
To make stock syrup for the gel, put sugar and water in a saucepan over a medium heat and stir until sugar is fully dissolved and liquid brought to boiling for about 2 minutes.

Pomegranate and beet gel
Strain the lemon juice and beetroot juice through some fine muslin cloth and put aside. In a pot combine the stock syrup and agar-agar, bring to a simmer and whisk for about 6 minutes. Gently warm the juice – do not boil. Gradually whisk the juice into the agar-agar and stock syrup, then add the pomegranate molasses. Pour into a shallow dish and refrigerate for about an hour to set. Remove from refrigerator and cut into manageable pieces, then purée in a blender, pass through a very fine sieve or fine-mesh tamis.

Vegetable garnish
Rehydrate the dried Chinese black fungus in water for 15–30 minutes, remove from water and pat dry on kitchen towel. Slice into very fine strips and lightly fry in oil with a small amount of butter.
Lightly blanch the halved asparagus spears in boiled salted water for about 1 minute and refresh in iced water.

Salmon
About 30 minutes before serving, place the wrapped ballotine and cubes of salmon in a water bath with a precise temperature of 50 °C / 122 °F and poach for about 20 minutes. Warm a suitable serving plate. Reheat the asparagus in a pan with some butter and lightly season with sea salt. Also reheat the Chinese black fungus and lightly season. Place the thin slice of beetroot on to the warmed plate. Remove the cooked salmon from the cling film and place on to the beetroot slice; place the smaller cubes randomly on to the plate. Add the asparagus in a decorative way along with the fried black fungus. Garnish with the pomegranate seeds and carefully spoon some of the beetroot gel randomly on to the plate and decorate with edible flowers. Serve straight away.

As this is close to a raw fish a Tokutei Meisho-Shu Sake would work a treat.

Photography Michael O'Meara

ceviche of salmon

Ceviche is a dish made using fresh raw fish marinated in citrus juices (typically lime or lemon) and spiced with chilli peppers, garlic, coriander and shallot. The acid from the citrus partially cooks the fish. I only use this recipe with fresh wild salmon.

serves 4

450 g / 1 lb wild salmon fillet, skinned
2 limes, juice only
1 shallot, finely sliced
1 teaspoon salt
1 fresh red chilli, de-seeded and very finely chopped
1 tablespoon olive oil

avocado salad
2 ripe avocados
3 firm tomatoes, peeled, de-seeded and diced
1 tablespoon lemon juice
2 tablespoons olive oil
pepper and salt
2 tablespoons fresh coriander leaves, chopped

Using a very sharp unserrated knife, cut the salmon fillet across into very thin strips, no thicker than 5 mm / ¼ inch (see note below).

Mix the lime juice, shallot and sea salt. Place the salmon in a non-metallic dish and pour over the lime juice mix, turning to make sure you coat all the strips with the juice.

Cover with cling film and leave refrigerated for at least an hour. Remove from fridge, add the chillis and a drizzle of oil, cover again and refrigerate.

Ensure you remove the ceviche from the fridge at least half an hour before serving so the salmon has time to get back up to room temperature, allowing the full flavour come to the fore.

Cut the avocados in half lengthways, remove the stones, peel and finely dice the flesh. Place in a bowl, pour the lemon juice over and mix gently.

Fold this into the tomatoes and olive oil. Season to taste. Cover with cling film and set aside.

Serve the salmon ceviche with avocado salad on four plates, garnished with coriander.

Note/Tip
To get very thin, even strips, make sure the salmon is very cold or place it in the freezer for about 10 minutes before you cut it.

Viognier, Condrieu, Burgundy. A top wine of the region. Well worth it for its elegant peachy flavours. Although a bit expensive, it has to be tasted at least once (and preferably several times) in a lifetime. The hint of honey marries beautifully with the limes, mild chilli and fish.

Chef **Aidan Mac Manus** *King Sitric* *Howth, Co. Dublin* kingsitric.ie
EURO-TOQUES

gravlax with mustard dressing

Wild salmon is of course the best but organic farmed salmon can also be very good. We have found that since farmed salmon is so readily available and relatively inexpensive, few customers are prepared to pay the extra money for wild seasonal salmon – but you pays for what you gets!

serves 10

gravlax
1 kg / 2 lb 4 oz salmon,
tail end, pin-boned
1 glass Irish whiskey
(approx. 35 ml / 1½ fl oz)
bunch fresh dill, chopped

marinade
50 g / 2 oz sugar
25 g/ 1 oz salt
25 g / 1 oz cracked black pepper
1 tablespoon allspice
1 tablespoon dried dill

mustard dressing
150 g / 5 oz sugar
110 mls / 4 fl oz water
1 teaspoon white wine vinegar
20 peppercorns
20 juniper berries
10 cloves
3 bay leaves
75 g / 3 oz Dijon mustard
75 g / 3 oz wholegrain mustard
bunch fresh dill, chopped

Mix all the marinade ingredients together.
Rub the marinade all over the salmon tail and place in a ziplock freezer bag.

Pour a glass of Irish whiskey over the salmon and add fresh dill. Close the bag and refrigerate, putting a weight on top. Leave for a minimum of 24 hours.

Over a medium heat, dissolve the sugar in water and white wine vinegar.

Add peppercorns, juniper berries, cloves and bay leaves. Simmer for a few minutes and remove from heat. Allow to cool. Strain.

Mix Dijon and wholegrain mustards with chopped fresh dill and add to the syrup.

To serve, wipe or wash the marinade off the salmon and slice thinly. Serve with the mustard dressing and some home-made brown bread (see p. 137).

Fino sherry, 'La Ina', Lustau, Jerez, Spain. Pleasantly dry with almond flavours, this suggestion should suit the palate. Unless you are tempted by a pint of Guinness or Murphy's, which go so well with whiskey tastes!

confit salmon, cucumber, bitter leaves and buttermilk

serves 4

350 g / 12 oz salmon loin, skinned and pin-boned
1 small cucumber
110 ml / 4 fl oz cider vinegar
bunch dill
50 ml / 2 fl oz water
500 ml / 16 fl oz olive oil
300 ml / ½ pint buttermilk
25 ml / 1 fl oz cream
2 leaves gelatin
12 g / ½ oz fresh horseradish
bitter leaves, such as chicory, dandelion, radish tops, watercress
beach herbs, such as arrow grass, sea radish
salt

Grate the horseradish into the buttermilk and cream and leave to infuse for 2 hours or longer.

Neatly trim the salmon into four fillets.
Peel and slice the cucumber into 12 neat slices and marinade in water, cider vinegar, salt and dill.

Strain the horseradish from the buttermilk and cream. Bloom the gelatin by placing it in ice cold water for 3–5 minutes, then squeeze to remove excess water and add to buttermilk and cream. Gently heat but do not boil as this destroys the gelatin's ability to set. Cool the liquid in a bowl over ice whisking continually until an airy foam forms.

Using a deep pan, preheat to 42–48 °C / 108–120 °F, ensuring there is enough olive oil to cover the salmon. Make sure the salmon is at room temperature before placing gently into oil. Do not allow the temperature of the oil to drop below 42 °C / 108 °F.
Cook the salmon for 14 minutes.

Pick and wash leaves and herbs, break up if necessary.

To serve, divide leaves and herbs among four plates. Add cucumber and a little marinade. Gently remove salmon from oil, drain on kitchen towel, season and place on leaves.
Season buttermilk gelatin and drizzle over the salmon.

Chardonnay, Constantia Uitsig, South Africa Initial flowers and citrus will combine with the herbs, leading on to a nutty fullness which is an ideal partner for buttermilk and horseradish.

natural history of Atlantic salmon

Our populations of wild Atlantic salmon are a gift from the sea. At the peak of the last Ice Age, some 24,000 years ago, we now know that Ireland and Britain were completely covered in a dense sheet of ice. As the ice slowly disappeared and Ireland was recolonised, one of the first invaders was the Atlantic salmon. Isolated in ice-free zones or refugia throughout the peak of this glacial age, different lineages of salmon invaded separate areas where the rivers were free from ice.

The Atlantic salmon is essentially a marine creature, using rivers and streams as a safe haven for its young but growing, feeding and maturing largely at sea. The great ocean journeys of the salmon are legendary, as is their uncanny ability to home accurately to their native rivers. This extraordinary navigational feat is accomplished through a combination of sensory perception, using well used tracks across the earth's magnetic fields, and a finely honed sense of smell or taste.

Research carried out over the past decade has for the very first time begun to map out the ocean corridors used for millennia by these amazing creatures and has given us an insight into how the small juvenile salmon, or smolts, are carried northwards in the surface layers of the great ocean currents.

It's sobering to think that practically none of the fish have any contact with their parents, and all of their highly developed senses are inbuilt in the tiny fertilised ovum. Included in this deceptively simple ball of cells is the basis for a sophisticated GPS tracking system which allows these creatures to navigate with ease the broad expanse of the North Atlantic, the ability to switch readily from living in fresh water to salt water, to recover fully, following spawning, from an advanced state of anorexia, and to recognise their exact place of birth. This incredible genetic endowment also allows them to ride ocean currents, climb the surging downthrust of giant waterfalls and forge upstream against the strongest of currents in some of the mightiest rivers on earth.

from fresh water to ocean and back again

Irish salmon are born in streams high up in the hills, live in freshwater until they are almost two years of age, then venture out to feeding grounds in the wide North Atlantic. They develop a silvery blue coat to adapt to their marine environment. Adult salmon return from the sea to breed in their native rivers. Once they approach shore waters the fish fan out and search for the taint or smell of their home river.

Not all salmon are equally successful in reaching their goal and some stray, wandering in and out of the estuaries and lower bays of neighbouring rivers. However, the bulk of the salmon make it back to their native river, and if the water levels are consistently high the fish can forge many tens of miles upstream in the first urgent dash towards their native streams, high in the hills. As water levels fall and the temperature rises, the salmon pause and rest in pools. Slowly, their flanks change colour from the brash silvery blue of their ocean coat to subtle browns and reds, far more in keeping with their autumnal freshwater surroundings.

Months go by and the salmon travel deeper and deeper into the freshwater catchment. Resting periods can span weeks or, in drought conditions, months. By mid-October the fish are fully mature, and with the first major floods of autumn they make a final dash towards their ancestral spawning grounds. Here, around Christmas week, they lay their eggs in banks of clean, silt-free gravel.

life cycle of the salmon

Image courtesy of the Atlantic Salmon Trust www.atlanticsalmontrust.org   ILLUSTRATION ROBIN ADE

The fertilised ova lie safe in their nests for 12 weeks or more. They develop surprisingly quickly, and within a few weeks the distinctive shape of the tiny fish is clearly visible moving about inside the soft, but tough, rubbery shell of the salmon egg, complete with dark, clearly differentiated eyes.

As the outline of the tiny salmon becomes even clearer, the nutrient-rich yolk of the egg forms into the tummy of the little fish. This yolk sac will provide the fry, or alevin, with all the sustenance it needs until it develops into a feeding fry. In most years, early April sees the hatching of the eggs and the appearance of tiny yolk sac fry, which lie deep in the egg nest or redd, in crevices among the stones, their fins constantly flicking about.

As they become more active, the tiny fish make their way to the surface of the redd, and by mid-April they are to be found on the bed of the stream. Once the yolk sac is fully absorbed the little fish become more active, set up territories and dart about the bed of the stream hunting incessantly for morsels of food.

The fry quickly develop distinctive 'thumbprints' along their flanks, which are characteristic of the young salmon, now known as salmon parr. In the spring of their second year, the parr develop a silvery coat, a clear indication that they are ready to take to the ocean. These salmon smolts quickly move downstream towards the ocean and the long journey north to their ancestral feeding grounds. **KW**

brunches & lunches

smoked salmon with soft-boiled egg and bagel

serves 2

110 g / 4 oz sliced smoked salmon
1 bagel, sliced in two halves
2 medium eggs
1 tablespoon butter
chives, finely chopped
salt and freshly ground
black pepper
2–3 tablespoons hollandaise
sauce (see p. 134)

Place the eggs in cold water, bring to the boil and cook for 1½–2 minutes, then plunge into a bowl of iced water.

Peel off shells when eggs have cooled. The best way to de-shell an egg is to start at the rounded end, not the peak end. The rounded end has a little air sac, and this makes it easier to peel the egg without damaging it.

Toast the bagel halves and butter when toasted.

Place buttered bagel halves on warmed plates, ruffle the smoked salmon on top and place a de-shelled egg on the salmon. Split the egg gently to allow the golden yolk spill over, season to taste and sprinkle with chives.

Serve the hollandaise sauce on the side.

An alternative is to fry instead of boil the eggs. For this, replace the hollandaise sauce with 1 teaspoon of creamed horseradish added to 1 tablespoon mayonnaise (see p. 134), mix well and spread on hot toasted bagel halves (no need to butter bagels). Place smoked salmon on each prepared bagel half, a softly fried egg on top, and dust with black pepper.

With brunch, try a Prosecco and freshly squeezed grapefruit cocktail: 70% Prosecco to 30% grapefruit is about right. With lunch, try a Grüner Veltliner, Loimer, Austria. Light with a delicious fruit finish.

salad of tea-smoked salmon with avocado, apple, celery, pistachio and spelt grain

Try smoking your own salmon using the method described below. Alternatively, buy the delicious Burren Smokehouse hot-smoked salmon.

serves 6–8

1 side of salmon, 700 g / 1½ lb, with skin, pin-boned
2 tablespoons water
1 tablespoon brown sugar
1 teaspoon salt

smoking
3 teaspoons tea leaves
or
2 tablespoons untreated sawdust
1 teaspoon sugar

salad
250 g / 9 oz mixed baby leaves, e.g. baby spinach, baby beetroot leaves, rocket, lamb's lettuce, little gem
1 avocado, sliced and tossed in some lemon juice
1 apple, sliced and tossed in some lemon juice
2 sticks celery, finely sliced
50 g / 2 oz shelled pistachios
110 g / 4 oz spelt grain, cooked
1 tablespoon pomegranate seeds
small bunch mint leaves

dressing
2 tablespoons groundnut oil
1 teaspoon rosewater
1 tablespoon passion fruit pulp
1 teaspoon honey
pinch salt

Salmon preparation and smoking

Mix the water with sugar and salt. Rub over the flesh side of the fish and leave to stand for 10 minutes before smoking.

Line a wok or roasting dish with enough foil to reach 4 cm / 1½ inches above the rim, flattening the foil firmly on the base and sides. Sprinkle the tea leaves or sawdust and the sugar in the base. Position an oiled rack above the tea leaves and place the fish, skin side down, on the rack. Make sure there is enough room above the fish for the air to circulate and smoke the fish thoroughly.

Cover the wok or roasting dish tightly with a lid and fold the overhanging foil in and around the edge of the lid to seal. Place wok or roasting dish on the stovetop over a high heat for 4–6 minutes (by this stage the mixture should be smoking vigorously), then reduce to a low heat and cook for a further 12 minutes. Turn off the heat but keep the lid closed for another 15 minutes so the fish absorbs the smoky flavours while it cools.

Dressing

Combine all the ingredients in a bowl or jar and stir to combine. Check for seasoning and adjust to taste.

Assembly

Arrange the salad leaves on a large platter and scatter over the avocado, apple, celery, pistachios, spelt grain, pomegranate seeds and mint leaves, reserving a few sprigs of mint for garnish.

Remove the skin from the salmon and flake the fish into large chunks with your hands.

Arrange on top of the salad ingredients on the platter.

Drizzle over the dressing and garnish with a few sprigs of mint.

Why not try a very good dry Cava, not too heavy or sleep-inducing: La Rosca, Cava, Brut, Spain.

wild salmon with sauce vierge

Wild salmon is a rare treat and this simple recipe allows the wonderful flavour of wild salmon to be enjoyed. Vary the herbs in the green sauce according to what is in season.

serves 4

4 wild salmon fillets,
175 g / 6 oz each, scaled (see p. 10)
and pin-boned
rapeseed oil, for frying

sauce vierge
110 ml / 4 fl oz extra virgin olive oil
1 lemon, juice only
2 tomatoes, skinned,
de-seeded, diced
1 shallot, finely diced
1 garlic clove, finely chopped
2 tablespoons baby capers
2 tablespoons fresh basil, torn
2 tablespoons fresh chervil,
chopped
2 tablespoons fresh dill, chopped
2 tablespoons fresh parsley,
chopped
2 tablespoons fresh chives,
snipped
salt and freshly ground black
pepper

Salmon
Heat a large frying pan; once hot, add the rapeseed oil.

Place the fillets of salmon skin side down on the pan and fry for 3 minutes.

Turn over and fry other side for another 3 minutes.

Remove the fillets from the pan and leave to rest in a warm place.

Sauce vierge
Pour the olive oil into a stainless steel pan.

Whisk in the lemon juice until well combined.

Add the chopped tomatoes, shallot, garlic and capers. Heat over a medium heat until the mixture is just warmed through.

Add the basil, chervil, dill, parsley and chives. Season to taste.

To serve, place a salmon fillet on each plate and spoon the sauce vierge over.

Serve with Irish baby potatoes and a dollop of real, creamy Irish butter.

Chardonnay, Saint-Aubin La Fontenette, Burgundy, France. This good value Bourgogne is from a very reputable producer, Marc Colin. Good clean, crisp lines of lime and mineral are in keeping with the natural flavours present here.

smoked salmon with spinach pappardelle pasta

serves 4

225 g / 8 oz smoked salmon, cut into strips
400 g / 14 oz dried spinach pappardelle
425 ml / ¾ pint cream
50 g / 2 oz butter
75 g / 3 oz Parmesan cheese shavings
black pepper, freshly ground
2 tablespoons capers, chopped
1 tablespoon wholegrain mustard
25 g / 1 oz smoked salmon strips, for garnish

Fill a large pot with water, add 1 teaspoon salt and bring to the boil. Cook the pasta in boiling water, stirring occasionally, until, al dente and strain well.

Melt the butter in a heavy-based pan, add cream, cheese shavings, capers, mustard and pepper. Mix and heat carefully until you have a smooth, even sauce.

Just before serving, add the salmon strips, gently tossing. Place the warm pasta in a heated bowl, pour sauce over and add some freshly ground pepper.

Garnish with smoked salmon strips.

Sauvignon Blanc, Pouilly-Fumé, 'Chatelain Prestige', Loire, France. This flinty and herbal wine is an excellent choice for pasta or potatoes with fish. If you want to test an all-time favourite, a Pinot Noir from the Gevrey-Chambertin region of Burgundy would further enrich the dish.

smoked salmon terrine

serves 8

225 g / 8 oz cold-smoked salmon
225 g / 8 oz hot-smoked salmon flaked
350 g / 12 oz soft cream cheese
2 tablespoons lemon juice
1 tablespoon grated lemon zest
1 tablespoon chives, finely chopped
1 tablespoon dill, finely chopped
1 large bunch watercress

Place all the ingredients except the salmon in a bowl or blender and process until nice and creamy.
Rub the inside of a small loaf or terrine tin with oil and line it with cling film, leaving extra cling film hanging over the edges.
Place the cold-smoked salmon along the bottom of the tin. Spoon a layer of the cheese and watercress mix into the tin. Lay a layer of the flaked hot-smoked salmon pieces on top. Continue layering until the tin is full. The final layer should be cold-smoked salmon covering the terrine neatly.
Fold the cling film over the top, press down gently for the terrine to take shape and set.
Chill for at least 8 hours or, if in a hurry, put in the freezer for at least 1 hour.
Remove the cling film before serving and slice on to a serving dish.
Garnish with some dill or watercress, with lemon wedges on the side.

Serve with ribbons of cucumber, sliced lengthways with a vegetable peeler, and dulse muffins (see p. 135)

Gamay, Morgon, Marcel et Mathieu Lapierre, Beaujolais Villages, France. A delicate light red wine, with the expected fruitiness on the palate, this should be an interesting match for the creamy cheese flavours. Fleurie, widely available, would also work.

hot-smoked salmon mini fishcakes with lemon butter sauce

Mini fishcakes are a hit with children and adults alike. Lemon butter sauce with its sharp, silky texture makes a delightful accompaniment.

makes 20 mini cakes

225 g / 8 oz hot-smoked salmon
225 g / 8 oz potatoes, cooked and mashed
50 g / 2 oz flour
1 egg, beaten (optional)
1 tablespoon butter, melted
1 lemon, zest and juice
1 lime, sliced for garnish
parsley, chopped
pinch salt and ground pepper
oil, for frying
lemon butter sauce (see p. 135)

Mix together the potatoes, flour, egg (if using), lemon zest and juice, melted butter and salt. Add the smoked salmon and parsley and mix.

Shape into about 20 small cakes, circles or triangles. Dust each with the peppered flour, fry in a little oil until golden on both sides. Drain on kitchen paper.

Serve while still hot, garnished with strips of smoked salmon, a sprinkle of parsley and a lime slice.

Riesling, Trocken, Geil, Rheinhessen, Germany. This fruity but light wine will combine with the sauce but is sturdy enough not to get lost.

salmon burgers

serves 4

450 g / 1 lb salmon fillets, skinned and de-boned
2 tablespoons fresh breadcrumbs
1 teaspoon fish sauce
1 teaspoon Dijon mustard
1 tablespoon minced onion
dash lemon juice
1 teaspoon coriander, chopped
a little oil and butter, for frying

Finely chop the salmon, place in a bowl with all the other ingredients and mix well.

Shape into 4 large burgers or 8 small burgers and refrigerate for about 30 minutes.

Fry on a hot heavy pan with a mix of oil and butter for about 2–3 minutes on either side until golden and crisp.

Serve with thinly sliced tomato, gherkin and red onion sprinkled with balsamic vinegar, or on a toasted open burger bun with some salad leaves and a tasty Marie Rose sauce (see p. 135).

Try a semi-chilled Gamay grape from Beaujolais Villages or a Cabernet-based Rosé d'Anjou, Loire, France. Both will merge with the exquisite mix of salmon and coriander.

Photography Harry Weir

cured Clare Island salmon with pear and mustard purée, fresh apple, pickled radish and shallot, citrus dressing

serves 4

600 g / 20 oz salmon fillet, skinned
750 ml / 25 fl oz water
150 g / 5 oz rock salt
275 g / 10 oz sugar
15g / ½ oz black peppercorns
7 star anise
5 cloves
4 juniper berries
½ tablespoon white wine vinegar
1 bunch coriander
1 fennel bulb, finely sliced

pear and mustard purée
2 pears
½ cinnamon stick
25g / 1 oz unsalted butter
concentrated mustard essence
salt

pickled radish and onion
1 shallot, peeled and finely sliced
(separate out 20 small rings)
2 radishes, finely sliced (you need
20 slices)
110 ml /4 fl oz apple cider vinegar
25g /1 oz sugar
generous pinch salt

citrus dressing
110 ml / 4 fl oz virgin olive oil
1 tablespoon lemon juice
1 tablespoon orange juice
1 tablespoon grapefruit juice
2–3 pinches salt
½ teaspoon sugar

apple discs
1 Granny Smith apple, peeled
and sliced

Cured salmon
Boil all ingredients, except salmon and fennel, until sugar and salt are dissolved.
Add the sliced fennel, take off the heat and leave to infuse.
When cool, completely submerge the salmon in the cure and leave for 6 hours.
Remove from the cure and allow to dry for 24 hours.

Pear and mustard purée
Peel and slice the pears. Melt butter, add pears, cook over high heat and
add the cinnamon stick. Cook for about 8 minutes.
Strain off liquid, remove cinnamon stick.
Liquidise the pear purée and pass through a chinois.
Pour into a squeezy bottle. Cool in a bowl of water in freezer.
Add concentrated mustard essence and salt to taste to finish.

Pickled radish and onion
In a small pan, bring the vinegar to the boil, add the sugar and salt, and stir to dissolve.
Remove from heat and allow to cool.
When cold, pour it over the radish and shallot and leave to marinate for 2 hours.

Citrus dressing
Place all ingredients together in a bowl and whisk.

Apple discs
Using a small disc-shaped cutter, cut 12 discs out of the apple slices.

Assembly
Place 3 slices of the cured salmon on each plate and 4–5 drops of the mustard and pear
purée. Add to this 3 apple discs per plate and some of the pickled radish and shallot.

Finish with the citrus dressing and some microgreens or baby leaves.

A good Pinot Grigio from Veneto such as 'Gregoris' 2012, Azienda Fattori. Ample, fleshy pear
flavour works brilliantly with the pear and mustard purée, and crisp citrus acidity cuts through
the rich flesh of the salmon to leave the palate refreshed.

salmon duo flan

serves 4–6

225 g / 8 oz fresh salmon, cubed
110 g /4 oz smoked salmon, diced
2 large eggs
2 egg yolks
300 ml / ½ pint heavy cream
1 onion, finely chopped
1 tablespoon chives, chopped
small knob of butter
salt and ground white pepper
pastry flan case (see p. 134)

Prepare and bake the pastry case for the flan first (see p. 134).

Preheat the oven to 190 °C / 375 °F / Gas mark 5.
Sauté the onion in the melted butter in a saucepan but do not allow to colour.
Toss in the fresh salmon and cook for 1–2 minutes. Leave aside to cool.

Beat the eggs and mix with the cream, seasoning and chives. Scatter the salmon cubes, onion and smoked salmon over the baked pastry base. Pour the egg and cream mix over the salmon and tilt to level the liquid.

Bake the flan in hot oven for 30–35 minutes until just set and golden on top.
Rest for a few minutes and serve warm with some chopped tomatoes and basil in dressing or a tossed green salad.

Chardonnay, Santaney, Domaine Borgeot, Burgundy, France. This is a reasonably priced white for this expensive wine region but still has enough fruit and mineral tones for this delicious dish. Worth it for the smell and taste of pears with the creamy salmon

smoked salmon on roasted baby potatoes

I love my potatoes and this is a wonderful way of serving a delicious combination for any gathering or celebration. Sinful but healthy! Even though potatoes are 80% water, they are a valuable source of vitamin C, protein, potassium, iron, thiamine, niacin and dietary fibre, with almost no fat. This recipe, which serves potatoes with the skin left on, is the very best way to eat them.

serves 4

225 g / 8 oz smoked salmon
25 g / 1 oz salmon roe or caviar
16 baby potatoes, even sized, washed and dried
2 tablespoons olive oil or rapeseed oil
1 tablespoon rosemary, chopped
1 tablespoon chives, chopped
3–4 tablespoons crème fraiche
sea salt and pepper
1 lemon, cut into 4 large or 8 small wedges

Preheat the oven to 200 °C / 400 °F / Gas mark 6. Toss the potatoes in the oil with rosemary and seasoning. Place on a hot tray and roast until potatoes are crisp on the outside and soft inside, about 30 minutes.

Leave to cool, then cut a cross on top of each and press open slightly.

Transfer to a serving plate, top each one with crème fraiche, then a piece of smoked salmon and roe. Garnish with the chopped chives and lemon wedges.

Sauvignon Blanc, Saint Clair, Marlborough, New Zealand. Zippy and razor sharp with a very clean finish. Will add the lemony flavours which taste so good with rosemary.

Kylemore Abbey salmon and spinach quiche

There is a wonderful array of ingredients to work with at Kylemore Abbey. Between the rich fishing in Pollacappul lough and the Victorian walled garden on site, it is any chef's dream. To see the salmon leaping in the lake in front of this iconic establishment, coupled with the quality and variety of herbs and vegetables produced in the garden, provides me with great inspiration to create dishes with a true taste of Connemara.

serves 8

base
275 g / 10 oz margarine
225 g / 8 oz cream flour
225 g / 8 oz wholemeal flour
4 tablespoons water
1 tablespoon fresh parsley, chopped
½ teaspoon salt
½ tsp pepper

filling
450 g / 1 lb fresh salmon, diced
450 g / 1 lb fresh spinach leaves, washed
1 teaspoon ground nutmeg
8 free range eggs
600 ml / 1 pint whole milk
600 ml / 1 pint cream
2 pinches dillisk flakes
salt and pepper to taste

Base
Preheat the oven to 180 °C / 350 °F / Gas mark 4.

Place flour, margarine, water, parsley, salt and pepper in a bowl and mix to form a firm dough. Knead until the dough is smooth and silky.

Put the dough in a freezer bag and refrigerate for at least 30 minutes.

Remove the dough from the fridge and roll on a floured work surface to 5 mm / ¼ inch thickness.

Place the pastry into a greased and floured 30 cm / 12 inch quiche tray and bake blind, weighed down with baking beans, for 16 minutes.

Remove from the oven and allow the base to cool while you prepare the filling.

Quiche
Preheat the oven to 150 °C / 300 °F / Gas mark 2.

Whisk together eggs, milk and cream with the ground nutmeg, salt, pepper and dillisk.

On the cooled quiche base, distribute the salmon and spinach evenly.

Pour the egg and milk mixture over the salmon and spinach and bake in the oven for 45 minutes.

Serve with freshly tossed green leaves and a three-bean salad.

A chilled glass of Pinot Grigio such as the full-flavoured organic Villa Teresa from Veneto, Italy, would work well with this quiche.

salmon with olives and tricolour quinoa

*Quinoa (pronounced **keen**-wah) is a grain-like seed that's full of protein and amino acids. There are a few different varieties, but white quinoa is the most common. It has a light, fluffy texture and a slightly nutty flavour. Red quinoa has a more pronounced nutty flavour; the black one is a little crunchier. They are sometimes sold as a blend, described as rainbow or tricolour quinoa.*

serves 4

4 salmon fillets, 175 g / 6 oz
each, skinned
175 g / 6 oz tricolour quinoa
1 red onion, finely sliced
2 cloves garlic, finely chopped
8 black olives, pitted and quartered
1 tablespoon capers, drained
2 tomatoes, skinned, de-seeded
and cubed
110 g / 4 oz rocket, washed
½ lemon, juiced
1 tablespoon olive oil
sunflower oil, for frying
½ teaspoon mixed peppercorns,
roughly ground
salt and pepper
fresh chives, finely chopped,
for garnish

Season salmon on both sides with salt and pepper. Oil and heat a non-stick sauté pan over a medium heat. Add salmon and cook on one side until golden brown, 3–4 minutes. Turn the fillets and cook for another 2–3 minutes until firm to the touch.

Prepare quinoa according to package directions. Season to taste with salt and pepper. Keep warm.

In a separate pan, heat sunflower oil over medium heat. Add onions and garlic and sauté until soft. Add the olives, capers, tomatoes, rocket, lemon juice and olive oil. Season to taste with salt and pepper.

Fold three-quarters of the olive and caper mix into the quinoa.

Using a ring mould or scone cutter, arrange a portion of the quinoa mix on each heated plate. Place the salmon fillet beside it.

Divide the remaining olive and caper mix between the plates and garnish with chopped chives and ground mixed peppercorns.

Sauvignon Blanc, Menetou-Salon, Domaine Chavet, Loire, France. An all-time favourite, this wine is floral and fruity but also crisp and refreshing. The crisp and fruity texture will be sublime with the salty olives and capers. The nutty quinoa will absorb all the flavours to perfection.

warm salmon salad

I originally tried this recipe with a pastrami of sea trout, a much smaller fish. The dish didn't really work as I was left with nectarine and cardamon with a faint taste of trout, so I decided to try salmon, which held its own against the nectarine and turned out to be a combo that really works.

Please note this is a dish utilising 'sous vide' cooking, i.e. the fish is sealed in cooking bags and vacuum-packed at a high pressure setting on the vac-pack machine. These machines usually run on a scale of 1–80, with 80 being the highest pressure setting. This ensures that the bag seals tightly around the fish, promoting more even cooking. Alternatively, the salmon could be pan-fried, poached or steamed.

serves 4

4 salmon fillets, 150 g / 5 oz each, skinned and pin-boned

10 ripe nectarines, skinned, de-seeded and roughly chopped

15 cardamom pods

110 g / 4 oz sugar

2 fennel bulbs

110 g / 4 oz fresh peas

2 packs or tubs pea shoots

8 red radishes

40 ml / 1½ fl oz lemon-infused olive oil

olive oil, for vacuum-cooking

Place the chopped nectarines in a pot with the sugar and sweat until very soft. Blend to a fine purée and infuse with crushed cardamom pods for an hour. Pass the purée through a fine sieve.

Place the salmon fillets in a small vacuum-pack bag with a teaspoon of olive oil and vaccum-pack on a medium-high pressure.

Cut the fennel into small wedges, put it in a vacuum-pack bag with lemon oil, reserving some lemon oil for dressing the radishes and peas. Vacuum-pack the fennel on the highest pressure. Steam it for 20–25 minutes and leave it in a warm place until serving.

Preheat a water bath to 55 °C / 130 °F, place the salmon in it and cook for 10 minutes.

Slice the radishes, pick the pea shoots, and blanch the fresh peas for 20 seconds. Dress all with remaining lemon oil and a pinch of salt.

Remove the salmon and fennel from the bags and arrange on the plates, adding a swipe of nectarine purée and the radish and pea garnish.

I am a big Alsace fan, so I suggest an Alsace Riesling such as Trimbach. The crisp flavour helps to cut through the oily salmon, and it works well with the subtle cardamom flavour.

mango salmon

Although I had worked as a chef on several continents and devoured delicious salmon from around the globe, it was not until I moved to Ireland with Móna in 2008 that I came to really understand this incredible fish and its fabulous flavours. Irish salmon in particular is in a league of its own, smoked, poached, seared or sashimi. In this recipe we aim for the sublime simplicity of sweet and sour alongside the salmon. Less here is most certainly more.

serves 4

4 salmon fillets, 200 g / 7 oz each,
with skin, pin-boned,
1 large ripe mango
1 lime
1 teaspoon chilli flakes
2 teaspoons salt
2 teaspoons black pepper,
coarsely ground
2 tablespoons olive oil,
for frying
1 bunch fresh coriander

Preheat the oven to 200 °C / 400 °F / Gas mark 6. Season the salmon fillets well with salt and coarsely ground black pepper. Choose a frying pan, preferably cast iron, that can go into the oven for final cooking.

Heat frying pan and when hot, add olive oil and sauté the salmon, skin side up, for 3 minutes. Finish the salmon in preheated oven for a further 10 minutes.

Make the salsa right before you serve.

Slice up the mango, mix with the juice of one lime and sprinkle salt and a few chilli flakes and a decent amount of coarsely chopped fresh coriander over the mango. This, in its simplest form, is the best way to eat a piece of fresh salmon.

We find this works deliciously with a crisp Grüner Veltliner from Austria or even a dry Riesling from Alsace.

spicy seared salmon with roasted fennel

serves 4

4 salmon fillets, 175 g / 6 oz each,
skinned

spicy marinade
4–6 star anise, crushed
4 tablespoons vermouth
1–2 teaspoons ginger, grated
1–2 cloves garlic, crushed
1 small red chilli, de-seeded and
finely chopped
2–3 tablespoons light soy sauce

fennel
2 fennel bulbs (thick base of stalk)
olive oil
1–2 tablespoons balsamic vinegar

Spicy marinade
Mix all the marinade ingredients and pour over the salmon fillets in a shallow dish. Brush the salmon on both sides with the marinade, cover and leave to stand for at least 2 hours. Pat the fillets dry with kitchen paper, place on a cast-iron ridged pan over a high heat and sear for 2–3 minutes on each side depending on thickness of fish.

Fennel
Preheat the oven to 200 °C / 400 °F / Gas mark 6. Halve the bulbs lengthwise and further subdivide into pieces about 25 mm / 1 inch thick. Coat with olive oil and sprinkle on some balsamic vinegar.
Lay out the fennel pieces on tinfoil and roast for 30–40 minutes or until cooked through and beginning to caramelise.

Serve with the salmon on four dinner plates.

Grüner Veltliner, Domäne Wachau, Austria. This is a fabulous wine from a well-respected vineyard. It will marry well with the fennel and spicy flavours. Slightly peppery and very succulent.

honeyed salmon skewers with noodles

I got this tasty and easy recipe from my daughter, who prepares it for her two young sons. They love the 'sticky' idea and they help by soaking the wooden skewers and threading the salmon. This is finger-licking good for children – and adults.

serves 4

12 long strips of salmon fillet, about 25 mm / 1 inch wide × 5 mm / ¼ inch thick
225 g / 8 oz egg noodles

marinade
1 tablespoon honey
2 tablespoons light soy sauce
1 tablespoon sunflower oil
1 tablespoon dry sherry
1 tablespoon Dijon mustard
1 tablespoon caster sugar
1 tablespoon lime juice
¼ red chilli, de-seeded and finely diced
1 teaspoon ginger, freshly grated

12 long skewers (if wooden, soak in water for 30 minutes to prevent scorching)

Mix all the marinade ingredients in a shallow bowl and submerge the salmon strips in the marinade.

Cover bowl with cling film and leave to marinate for a minimum of 10 minutes.

Heat the grill to a high setting, or if using a ridged pan, heat and oil it. Thread the salmon strips on the soaked skewers in zig-zag shape and cook quickly for 1–2 minutes only on each side.

Simmer the marinade in a small pot and reduce slightly. Keep warm.

Just before serving, prepare noodles according to package directions. Drain well and place in a warmed bowl.

Divide noodles between four plates and place salmon skewers on top. Drizzle the salmon skewers with the warmed marinade to glaze.

Sauvignon Blanc, Wither Hills, Marlborough, New Zealand. This wine is lively on the palate with herbal and lemony flavours. A Riesling, Sipp Mack, Alsace, France, would be an equally good partner for the marinade.

chargrilled salmon with ribbon courgettes and cherry tomatoes

serves 4

4 salmon fillets, 175 g / 6 oz each, skinned
12 cherry tomatoes, halved
2 medium-sized courgettes
olive oil, for frying
sea salt and freshly ground pepper

marinade
1 tablespoon Dijon mustard
2 teaspoons honey
1 tablespoon root ginger, grated
1 tablespoon garlic, crushed
1 tablespoon light soy sauce
2 tablespoons olive oil

In a large non-metallic dish, arrange the salmon to fit comfortably in a single layer. Mix all the marinade ingredients and pour over the fish, cover with cling film and leave aside for 15–30 minutes.

While salmon is marinating, slice the courgettes lengthways into fine ribbons, place in ice-cold water until ready to cook, then drain and pat dry

When ready to cook, remove the salmon fillets from the marinade. Grill the fillets under a hot grill until charred on both sides, about 3 minutes per side depending on thickness. Test with your finger for firmness.

Heat the olive oil on a ridged pan and fry the courgette ribbons for a few minutes only until they are nicely browned. Remove from the heat and keep hot. Add the halved tomatoes to the hot ridged pan and char.

Serve the salmon on warm plates with courgette ribbons and charred tomaotes.

Muscadet de Sèvres et Maine, Loire, France. Packed with delightful fruit and a crisp dryness to the palate. Make sure the Muscadet is 'sur lie'; it costs a little more but is worth it.

smoked salmon and poached egg with colcannon cake

serves 2

2 slices of smoked salmon
2 fresh eggs
1 tablespoon white wine vinegar
110 g / 4 oz potatoes, cooked and mashed
75 g / 3 oz butter, melted
25 g / 1 oz savoy cabbage, finely shredded
1–2 scallions, finely chopped
salt and black pepper
flour to coat colcannon cakes
vegetable oil to fry colcannon cakes
2–3 tablespoons hollandaise sauce (see p. 134)

Sauté the scallions and cabbage in 50 g / 2 oz butter until tender.
Fold the cabbage mix into the mashed potatoes, add 25 g / 1 oz butter and season.
Shape this colcannon mix into 2 nice patties using some flour to help shape and coat.
Heat the oil in a hot pan and fry the patties on both sides for 3–4 minutes until golden. Cover and keep warm.
To poach the eggs, bring a large pot of water with salt to the boil and add 1 tablespoon vinegar. Crack the eggs, one at a time, into a small bowl or plate and gently slide into the simmering water. Ensure you do not break the yolk. Simmer for about 3–4 minutes until just cooked and yolks soft. Remove with slotted spoon, drain well and set aside on a warm saucer.
Heat the smoked salmon for 1–2 minutes on a hot pan.
Place each colcannon cake on a hot serving plate, put a slice of smoked salmon on the cake and top with poached egg.

Spoon over some hollandaise sauce and add a grinding of black pepper.

Prosecco frizzante, Bartolomiol, Italy. A light sparkling wine from the Glera grape. Perfect for brunch.

Chef **Patrick Howard** *Abbeyglen Castle Hotel* *Sky Road, Clifden, Co. Galway* abbeyglen.ie

spiced salmon and minted cucumber

Any cut of salmon may be used for this dish. Sprinkle as much or as little spice on to your salmon to suit your own taste.

serves 8

8 salmon fillets, 225 g / 8 oz each,
4 cucumbers, peeled and
de-seeded
110 g / 4 oz fresh mint, finely
chopped
250 ml / 9 fl oz olive oil
1 teaspoon red wine vinegar
½ lemon, juice
piri-piri
cajun seasoning
clarified butter, for frying
pepper and salt to season
8 cherry tomatoes
110 g / 4 oz rocket, washed

Grate the cucumber and cover with olive oil.
Add red wine vinegar, lemon juice and mint to the cucumber mixture.
Taste and season as necessary.
Refrigerate to chill, overnight if possible.

Preheat the oven to 180 °C / 350 °F / Gas mark 4.
Mix the piri-piri with the cajun seasoning and coat the salmon fillets.
Heat a pan with clarified butter until very hot. Carefully sear both sides of the salmon for approximately 2 minutes on both sides.
Remove from the heat and finish cooking in the oven for a further 10 minutes.

To serve, place the salmon in the centre of plate and top with the chilled minted cucumber.
Garnish with cherry tomato and rocket.

Sauvignon Blanc, Churton, Marlborough, New Zealand. This full-bodied Sauvignon, with tropical notes, will hold its own with the spiced salmon. If, like me, you enjoy Riesling with spices, try the Urgestein, Schloss Gobelsburg, from Austria, with its lime aromas and mineral and flower textures.

Dr **Máirtín Mac Con Iomaire** *School of Culinary Arts and Food Technology* *Dublin Institute of Technology, Dublin 1* dit.ie

smoked salmon with poppy seeds and horseradish-infused crème fraiche

serves 4

150 g / 5 oz smoked salmon,
sliced
1 teaspoon poppy seeds
50 ml / 2 fl oz crème fraiche
1 teaspoon horseradish cream
salt and pepper

garnish
mixed lettuce leaves, washed
sprig of fresh dill or fennel

Combine the crème fraiche and the horseradish cream and mix.
Season to taste with a little salt and pepper.
Reserve in the fridge until required.
To serve, select a suitable sized plate and arrange a little smoked salmon around
the outside of the whole plate.

In the centre of the plate place a small handful of mixed lettuce leaves.
Try to get a little structure and height into the garnish.
Sprinkle poppy seeds over the smoked salmon.
Finally, pour horseradish cream into the centre of the lettuce and top with
a sprig of fennel or dill.

Viognier, Willunga 100, McLaren Vale, Australia. The honeysuckle and stone fruit notes will add a touch of sweetness to balance the flavours.

double-marinated Mourne Seafood salmon pastrami with pickled fennel and wasabi crème fraiche

The salmon undergoes two separate cures in this recipe, each lasting 24 hours. The double marination produces subtle flavours. The cured salmon will keep for two days if refrigerated and well wrapped. Prepare all the garnishes well in advance so that all you have to do is decorate the plates and serve.

serves 4

360 g / 12 oz salmon fillet, skinless and pin-boned
50 g / 2 oz dill, finely chopped

first marinade
1 tablespoon coriander seeds
1 tablespoon star anise
1 tablespoon fennel
50 g / 2 oz coarse sea salt
50 g / 2 oz sugar
½ orange, juice and rind
salt and pepper, freshly ground

second marinade
2 tablespoons Dijon mustard
1 teaspoon dill, finely chopped
1 teaspoon lemon balm, finely chopped
1 teaspoon coriander, finely chopped
1 teaspoon chervil, finely chopped

wasabi crème fraiche
50 g / 2 oz crème fraiche
½ teaspoon wasabi

pickled fennel
2 fennel bulbs, thinly sliced
110 ml / 4 fl oz water
110 ml / 4 fl oz white wine vinegar
110 g / 4 oz sugar
50 m / 2 fl oz olive oil

First marinade
Mix all the ingredients for the first marinade and place on cling film.

Place the salmon in the marinade and cover it well. Seal in the cling film and place in the fridge for 24 hours.

Next day, remove the salmon and scrape any remaining marinade away. Set aside.

Second marinade
Mix all the marinade ingredients and repeat the process as before for a further 24 hours.

Wasabi crème fraiche
Mix together the wasabi and crème fraiche. Chill until ready to use.

Pickled fennel
Warm the water, white wine vinegar, sugar and olive oil together. When warmed, pour over the fennel slices and allow to infuse.

When ready to serve, oil some cling film and shake the finely chopped dill over it.

Cover the presentation side of the salmon with the dill by placing the salmon down on the coated cling film.

Slice the salmon into four portions and serve with the pickled fennel and droplets of the wasabi crème fraiche to the side.

Spicy Japanese elements, particularly wasabi, make for a difficult match with wine. A small bottle of sake, warmed in a container of warmed water, makes a good accompaniment. A good wine choice is Viognier, preferably from the Northern Rhône. The best Viognier has a creamy, floral waxiness, with a touch of apricots and peaches, which will help it wrap around the crème fraiche without overwhelming the salmon.

beetroot- and grapefruit-cured wild salmon with beets, nettle mayonnaise and rye crispbread

Salmon is a very versatile and forgiving ingredient: grilled, roasted, poached or, as in this case, cured, it is an appealing and always popular choice. The cured salmon in this dish is almost meat-like and is enhanced by the earthy beetroot crisp, the nettle mayonnaise and the slightly pickled beetroot paint, which cuts through the rich oiliness of the fish. Finally, the rye crispbread lends a nice textural change.

serves 4

cured salmon
300 g / 11 oz wild salmon,
trimmed and pin-boned
½ pink grapefruit, zest and juice
1 large organic beetroot, peeled
15 g / ½ oz sea salt flakes
15 g / ½ oz brown sugar
pinch crushed white peppercorns
15 g / ½ oz lemon thyme,
chopped

sugar syrup
75 ml / 3 fl oz water
50 g / 2 oz sugar

beets
1 large beetroot
50 ml / 2 fl oz sugar syrup
25 ml / 1 fl oz white wine vinegar
25 g / 1 oz sugar
110 ml / 4 fl oz water

nettle mayonnaise
50 g / 2 oz young nettles
110 g / 4 oz mayonnaise
(see p. 134)
½ lemon, juice

eggs
4 quail eggs
or
4 small hen eggs

8 slices rye bread (see p. 136)

Cured salmon
Mix sugar, salt, peppercorns, pink grapefruit zest and lemon thyme together. Chop the beetroot and blend with the grapefruit juice in a food processor until a paste is formed. Spread the sugar and thyme mixture on both sides of the salmon, then rub the beetroot and grapefruit paste on the salmon. Wrap the salmon in clingfilm and place in a fridge for a minimum of 3 days. When you're ready to use, unwrap and gently rinse under cold water. Slice as required.

Sugar syrup
Put water and sugar in small saucepan and cook until sugar is fully dissolved and the liquid is of a medium thick consistency.

Beets
Cut six thin slices from the large beetroot. Brush the beetroot slice with the sugar syrup and place on parchment paper. Dry in a very cool oven until crisp. Chop the remainder of the beetroot and boil with the vinegar, sugar and water. When the beetroot is tender blend with a stick blender and pass through a fine strainer. Chill the beetroot syrup.

Nettle mayonnaise
Blanch the young nettle leaves in boiling salted water for a few seconds. Refresh nettles by plunging into iced water. Squeeze the nettle leaves to remove excess moisture and place in a blender with the mayonnaise. Blend into a smooth paste and correct the seasoning with lemon juice.

Eggs
Boil quail eggs for 2 minutes, remove from hot water and refresh under cold water. When cool enough to handle, remove the shell. If using hen eggs, place in cold water, bring to the boil and time for 3 minutes from when water starts to boil. Refresh under cold water, and when cool enough to handle, remove the shell.

To serve, arrange the sliced salmon on a chilled plate with toasted thin slices of rye bread, beetroot crisp, and beetroot paint, arrange the soft boil egg between the slices and finish with a dollop of nettle mayonnaise.

Manzanilla, 'La Gitana', Hidalgo, Barrameda, Spain. Provided it is chilled and freshly opened, the tangy, salty sherry, although traditionally an aperitif, makes an ideal accompaniment to the challenging, delicious flavours present here.

salmon, spinach and pine nut filo tart

serves 6

400 g / 14 oz fresh salmon, cooked and cooled

1 small onion, diced

2 garlic cloves, chopped

200 g / 7 oz spinach leaves, spine removed, washed and roughly chopped

1 tablespoon olive oil

salt and pepper

pinch nutmeg

2 tablespoons fresh dill, chopped (or 2 teaspoons dried dill)

1 tablespoon fresh mint, chopped (or 1 teaspoon dried mint)

2 tablespoons fresh flat-leaf parsley, chopped (or 2 teaspoons dried parsley)

110 g / 4 oz mozzarella cheese, grated

50 g / 2 oz Parmesan cheese, grated

50 g / 2 oz pine nuts, toasted

3 eggs

6 sheets filo pastry

25 g / 1 oz melted butter

Filling

Sauté the onion and garlic in the olive oil in a large saucepan over medium to high heat.

Once the onion has softened and the garlic is fragrant, add the spinach and stir, cooking for about 5 minutes until all the moisture has evaporated.

Season with salt, pepper and nutmeg and add the chopped herbs. Remove from the heat and cool. Flake the cooked salmonand add to the mix, with the grated cheese and toasted pine nuts. Taste for seasoning.

In a separate bowl, whisk the eggs and then add to the filling, mixing carefully to combine.

Tart

Preheat the oven to 170 °C / 325 °F / Gas mark 3.
Melt the butter and use a pastry brush to grease a 30 cm / 12 inch pie tin.

Place the defrosted filo pastry on a clean worktop and cover with a damp cloth to keep it fresh while you work with it. Working one sheet at a time, brush each sheet with butter and layer into the tart tin, pushing into the sides and overlapping so that the overhang is even all around the tart. Don't worry about any pieces that break, they will be overlapped with more sheets of filo.

Add the filling into the tart and crumple the overhanging pastry along the edge to create a pretty crumpled paper effect. Bake for 25 minutes on the middle rack of the oven. Before removing, ensure that the filling has set by giving the tart a light touch; it should be firm and not wet.

To serve, slice carefully into wedges using a long serrated knife and accompany with salad.

Sauvignon Blanc, Bellow's Rock, Western Cape, South Africa. Tropical and citrus fruits coupled with a crisp acidity. Nice for lunch.

blackened Irish salmon with fresh cucumber, mango and herb salad, served with pepper and soy dressing

We are so lucky in Ireland to have such availability of wonderful fresh salmon. The warmer, highly oxygenated waters supplied by the North Atlantic Drift make for a much fuller flavour, perfect fat content and a great colour. Salmon is so versatile – it can be poached, grilled, baked, cured, smoked, and in this recipe you can even burn it! I have prepared a vibrant dish that is perfect for a light lunch or starter, with Irish salmon as the star.

serves 6

6 salmon fillets, 150 g / 5 oz each, skinned
1 cucumber
1 ripe mango
4 spring onions
25 g / 1 oz fresh mint
25 g / 1 oz fresh basil
25 g / 1 oz fresh coriander
1 red pepper, finely diced
1 lime
4 tablespoons soy sauce

Place the diced pepper in a bowl with the soy sauce.

Peel the cucumber lengthways into ribbons, turning it on each peel until you get to the middle (do not use the seedy part) and place in a salad bowl.

Thinly slice the spring onions at a slight angle and add to the cucumber ribbons. Roughly chop all of the herbs, including the stalks, and add to the salad bowl. Peel the mango into ribbons over the bowl, making sure to catch the juice. Zest the lime and squeeze the juice into the salad, carefully mixing together with your hands.

Rub a little oil all over the salmon and place it presentation side down on a very hot frying pan. It will smoke a bit but do not move the salmon and cook for approx. 5 minutes until it is charred. Turn it over and cook for approx. 3 more minutes. Place on a dish, take some of the soy sauce that the peppers have been marinated in and spoon over the salmon every now and again. Leave to rest for about 30 minutes.

To serve, place portion of salad on each plate, spoon the peppers and a little of the soy sauce on the side and place the salmon fillet on top of the salad.

As an alternative cooking method, you could barbecue the salmon whole. Clean and gut the salmon, wash well under a running cold tap, pat dry with kitchen towel and lightly oil the skin. Place salmon on the shiny side of tinfoil, wrap well and barbecue until blackened. Serve whole on top of the salad.

Our head sommelier, David Gallagher, recommends Château La Canorgue Viognier, Pays du Vaucluse, Rhône, France. A heady wine with aromas of apricots and white peach, its fruity and floral characteristics perfectly complement the fresh salad. The crisp acidity acts as a marvellous foil to the rich, charred salmon.

pressed terrine of Kenmare Select organic salmon with pink grapefruit, coriander and basil

serves 8

terrine

800 g / 1 lb 12 oz side Kenmare
Select organic smoked salmon,
thinly sliced
225 g / 8 oz unsalted butter,
softened
2 tablespoons horseradish sauce
2 tablespoons fresh parsley,
chopped
salt and pepper

grapefruit

4 pink grapefruit, peeled, zest cut
into fine strips, segments halved
1 pink grapefruit, juice only
50 ml / 2 fl oz champagne vinegar
25 g / 1 oz sugar
14 coriander seeds, lightly crushed
8 basil leaves, cut into fine strips

Soften the butter and blend in the food processer until smooth.

Add the lemon juice and horseradish sauce and blend. Place the mixture in a bowl and beat in the capers and chopped parsley. Season with salt and pepper to taste.

Line a terrine mould with cling film and build up thin layers of the smoked salmon and soft butter mix.

Press the terrine by placing a weight on top and leave overnight. The terrine can be stored in the fridge for up to three days.

For the pink grapefruit, place the vinegar, sugar, coriander seeds, grapefruit juice and zest in a saucepan.

Place over a medium heat and reduce (see p. 12) by two-thirds until there is a syrup consistency. When cool, pour it over the grapefruit segments, add the basil and store in the fridge.

To serve, slice the terrine with a very sharp knife and arrange slices on plates.

Surround with the syrup-coated grapefruit segments.

IMAGE MARK DOE

Sauvignon Blanc, Morton Estate, Marlborough, New Zealand. The combination of grapefruit and herbs with the fish needs a wine assertive enough to deal with this scrumptious terrine. Passion fruit and hints of lime in this dry, full wine will add more excitement to the palate.

potted salmon

As part of an RTÉ Lyric FM series 'History on a Plate', I recreated some old Irish dishes. They ranged in style but, interestingly, they had exceptionally good flavour and the combinations were classical in a modern way. The original recipe on which this dish is based is from 'Mrs Jane Bury her receipt booke, 1700', a manuscript which I found in the National Library of Ireland (Townley Hall Papers). Fascinating stuff.

serves 4–6

200 g / 7 oz butter
1 kg / 2 lb 4 oz salmon fillet,
with skin, pin-boned
few scrapes nutmeg
4 cloves
½ teaspoon mace
½ teaspoon cinnamon
½ teaspoon ground ginger
1 tablespoon sea salt
black pepper

Preheat the oven to 160 °C / 325 °F / Gas mark 3.

Generously butter a gratin dish that will hold the salmon in one piece, using half the butter.

Place the salmon skin side up in the dish. Using a pestle and mortar, mix a good few scrapes of nutmeg and the 4 cloves, along with the mace, cinnamon, ginger, sea salt and pepper.

Mix it thoroughly until you have a well-seasoned salt.

Score the salmon skin lightly in a few places and then sprinkle the salt on to the skin.

Dot with the remaining butter, cover with parchment paper and then wrap tightly in foil.

Place foil-wrapped salmon in oven and bake for 30–40 minutes, depending on how well done you like the salmon.

Remove from the oven and leave to rest for 10 minutes. Remove the foil and parchment paper with care as steam will come out.

Scrape off excess salt and remove the skin.

Portion the cooked salmon carefully on to plates, taste and season if needed.

Drizzle with some of the butter from the gratin dish.

Serve with boiled potatoes and some samphire.

A delicious white burgundy or possibly an artisan cider would be great with this rich and buttery salmon dish. It would also stand up to a more complex white such as a Condrieu or a white Châteauneuf-du-Pape.

poached salmon with sorrel cream

serves 4

4 salmon fillets, 175 g / 6 oz each,
de-scaled and pin-boned,
6 carrots, peeled and cut lengthways
star anise
½ lemon, juice
½ glass white wine
1 bay leaf
1 sprig dill
10 white peppercorns
1 litre / 1¾ pints water
salt

sorrel cream
1 small shallot, finely diced
400 ml / 14 fl oz fish stock
(see p. 136)
150 ml / 5 fl oz dry white wine
200 ml / 7 fl oz double cream
salt and pepper
½ lemon, juice
bunch sorrel leaves, torn

garnish
2 lemons, cut in wedges
1 tablespoon olive oil

Cook the carrots in seasoned water until soft. Put 1 litre of water in a large pot, add the star anise, lemon juice, white wine, bay leaf, dill, peppercorns and salt and bring to the boil. Reduce the heat and add salmon and cook slowly for 6–8 minutes. Do not stir and do not allow to boil. Remove the salmon from the liquid and place on cloth to remove excess liquid.

Sorrel cream
Place the diced shallot in a pan with the fish stock and wine, bring to boil and reduce by half (see p. 12). Once reduced, add the cream and season with salt, pepper and lemon juice. Add in the torn sorrel leaves.

To serve, rub the salmon skin with olive oil and place fillet on each of four plates. Place the carrots on the side and pour over the sorrel cream. Garnish with lemon wedges.

Sauvignon Blanc Semillon, Cullen Mangan Vineyard, Australia. Crisp lime and lemon with a herby finish will do justice to the cream-sauced fish.

Food Consultant **Colin O'Daly** *Parknasilla Resort & Spa* *Sneem, Co. Kerry* parknasillahotel.ie

roast wild salmon with fresh herbs on bed of samphire

I love the story of Fionn and how, when faced with a problem, he had only to suck his thumb to get access to the knowledge gifted to him by the salmon. This very simple dish, which is gluten-, dairy- and wheat-free, pays homage to the fish of knowledge, the glorious Irish salmon.

serves 8

1 kg / 2 lb 4 oz fillet wild Irish salmon, with skin, pin-boned
mixed herbs, tarragon, chives, dill, chopped
sea salt
black pepper
1 tablespoon olive oil
1 lemon, juice and zest
1 clove garlic (optional)
olive oil, to coat baking tray

samphire
225 g / 8 oz marsh samphire, tough stems removed
2 tablespoons butter
1 lemon, juice
black pepper, freshly ground
2 litres / 3½ pints water

Preheat the oven to 200 °C / 400 °F / Gas mark 6.
Combine the tablespoon of olive oil with the herbs, lemon juice and zest in a food processor and blend until you have a fine paste.
Drizzle olive oil on the baking tray with crushed clove of garlic, if using.
Place the salmon on the tray skin side down, and spread the herby paste over the salmon flesh. Sprinkle sea salt and black pepper over the salmon.
Place the salmon in the oven and cook for 10–15 minutes.

Samphire
Bring 2 litres of water to the boil and add the samphire, return to the boil for 2–3 minutes, until tender. Remove the samphire and drain well. Melt butter in pan over medium heat and add samphire and lemon juice. Season, to taste, with black pepper.

Remove the skin from the salmon fillet and divide into 8 portions.
Serve on warmed plates with buttered samphire in the centre and salmon placed on top.

Chablis, 'Fourchaume', Domaine Denis Race, Burgundy, France. Floral and fruity, with hints of mineral and chalk, this is a classic accompaniment for a classic dish.

Photography Julia Dunin

organic salmon, trout roe, pickled cucumber, dill oil

serves 4

salmon and trout roe
4 salmon fillets, 110 g / 4 oz each,
pin boned
1 small jar trout roe
sea salt

dill oil
bunch of dill
250 ml / 9 fl rapeseed oil

pickled cucumber
1 cucumber, thinly sliced
(a mandolin will help)
1 cucumber, peeled and cut into
1cm / ⅜ inch rounds
250 ml / 9 fl oz cider vinegar
175 g / 6 oz sugar

garnish
sea salt flakes
some small baby bitter leaves,
such as watercress, kale, radish or
kohlrabi

equipment
small food thermometer

Dill oil
Blanch the dill in simmering water for 1–2 minutes and plunge immediately into iced water.
Dry the dill completely and place in a small pot.
Cover with the oil and warm to 60 °C / 140 °F for 8 minutes.
Pour into a container and allow to infuse for a few hours.
Strain before use.

Pickled cucumber
Heat the sugar and vinegar in a small pot until the sugar has dissolved.
Allow the pickle to cool.
Put both kinds of cucumbers into a bowl and mix together, pour cooled pickle over
and refrigerate until required.

Salmon
Season the salmon lightly with sea salt.
Place the fillets in four separate ziplock freezer bags.
Ensure as much air as possible is removed before sealing.
Cook the salmon in 44 °C / 110 °F water for 12 minutes.

Assembly
Remove the salmon from the bags carefully.
Place on the plate and arrange three cucumber rounds on each side of the salmon.
Curl one cucumber strip and place upright on the plate.
Place a little bit of the roe on top of each salmon fillet.
Dress with the dill oil.
Finally decorate with the baby bitter leaves and season with some salt flakes.

A nice Albariño from Galicia (Spain) would go well with this salmon dish. Its fruity and
slightly floral character will pick up and complement the subtle notes of the trout roe
and the bitter leaves.

Chef **Graham Roberts** *Connemara Smokehouse* Ballyconneely, Connemara, Co. Galway smokehouse.ie

Mawky's smoked salmon quiche

Connemara Smokehouse has been operating since 1979. Honouring traditional methods, we use beechwood smoke to produce smoked salmon of exceptional quality. Mawky was my grandmother who passed away some years ago. She was a great cook. This salmon quiche was one of her signature dishes, and it continues to be a firm favourite in the Roberts household.

serves 4–6

pastry base
225 g / 8 oz plain flour
110 g / 4 oz butter
1 egg
1 egg yolk

filling
225 g / 8 oz Connemara
Smokehouse smoked salmon
3 large eggs
350 ml / 12 fl oz cream (or half
cream, half milk for lighter filling)
½ lemon, juice
2 tablespoons fresh parsley,
chopped

You will need a 25.5 cm / 10 inch quiche or flan tin (preferably metal) with fluted edge and removable base.

Preheat the oven to 200 °C / 400 °F / Gas mark 6. For the pastry base, beat egg and egg yolk well. Slice butter into thin slices and mix into eggs. Add flour gradually, working it into a thick paste. Roll out to size of quiche or flan tin, pressing pastry firmly into tin.

Cover bottom of pastry-lined tin with thin slices of smoked salmon (using about half the fish) and leave in the fridge for 15 minutes. To make the filling, beat the eggs and add cream (or milk and cream), chopped parsley and lemon juice.
Chop the remainder of the salmon into small cubes and add to egg mixture.
Pour filling into pastry-lined tin and bake in oven for 25–30 minutes until quiche is set in the centre, has turned golden brown and looks puffy.

Serve with a nice green salad.

Gamay, Domaine des Nugues, Beaujolais Villages, France. Top producer Gérard Gelin is responsible for this light red wine with red berry aroma and taste. The low-tannin style will not overpower this delicious, classic quiche.

baked salmon with hazelnuts and apple syrup

I recently discovered Highbank Orchard Syrup, produced by Highbank Organic Farm in Cuffesgrange, Co. Kilkenny. It has a delightfully sweet and fragrant apple taste which works extremely well with salmon. The association with hazelnuts, as in this recipe, was inspired by the poem 'The Song of Wandering Aengus' by W.B. Yeats.

serves 2

2 salmon fillets, 175 g / 6 oz each, skinned
1 tablespoon dried breadcrumbs
1–2 tablespoons wholegrain mustard
50 g / 2 oz hazelnuts, crushed
1 teaspoon dill, finely chopped
1–2 teaspoons Highbank Orchard syrup (or maple syrup or honey)
3–4 tablespoons apple juice

Preheat the oven to 200 °C / 400 °F / Gas mark 6.

Mix the crumbs, mustard, hazelnuts and dill in a bowl, add 1 teaspoon apple syrup and enough apple juice to bind the mixture.

Place the salmon fillets on a piece of parchment paper, press the crumb mix on to the fillet and drizzle a little more syrup over the top.

Bake in the top of the oven for about 10–12 minutes, depending on thickness.

Serve on warmed plates with a creamy mash.

Colombard-Ugni Blanc, Domaine Uby, Gascony, France. This good-value wine is full of apricots and peaches to the nose and on the palate. It is not too sweet and will pleasantly unite the contrasting flavours of nut, mustard and apple.

excerpt from

The Song of Wandering Aengus

W.B. YEATS

I went out to the hazel wood,
Because a fire was in my head,
And cut and peeled a hazel wand,
And hooked a berry to a thread;
And when white moths were on the wing,
And moth-like stars were flickering out,
I dropped the berry in a stream
And caught a little silver trout.
...
And walk among long dappled grass,
And pluck till time and times are done
The silver apples of the moon,
The golden apples of the sun.

Frank Hederman's beech-smoked salmon with quenelle of crab and cauliflower tempura

serves 4

110 g / 4 oz beech-smoked salmon

quenelle of crab
225 g / 8 oz white crab meat, picked over to remove any pieces of shell
½ red chilli, deseeded and very finely chopped
1 lime, zest
1 pink grapefruit, segmented, chopped, sieved to remove excess juice
1 orange, segmented, chopped, sieved to remove excess juice
8 mint leaves, finely shredded
2 tablespoons mayonnaise (see p. 134)
salt
white pepper, freshly ground

avocado purée
1 avocado, peeled and stoned
1 tablespoon crème fraiche
pinch of cayenne pepper
½ lime, juice only
salt
white pepper, freshly ground

cauliflower tempura
50 g / 2 oz cornflour, sifted
2–3 tablespoons iced water
4 cauliflower pieces, 35 g / 1½ oz each
salt
white pepper, freshly ground

Salmon
Using a long, straight-edged knife, slice thin horizontal slices from the smoked salmon. Cut these layers into even squares 4 cm / 1½ inch × 4 cm / 1½ inch.

Quenelle of crab
Mix the crab meat, chilli, lime, grapefruit, orange and mint in a bowl. Fold in the mayonnaise and season to taste. Pack the crab mixture into four 8 cm / 3 inch cylindrical moulds. Lift off the mould.

Avocado purée
Blend the avocado, crème fraiche, cayenne pepper and lime juice in a food processor. Season to taste.

Cauliflower tempura
Add the water to the cornflour in a bowl and whisk until a batter consistency is achieved. Preheat the deep-fat fryer to 170 °C / 340 °F.

Bring a medium-sized saucepan of water to simmering point and plunge the cauliflower into it for a few seconds. Drain the cauliflower and refresh in a bowl of ice-cold water. Drain again.

Dip the cauliflower in the batter, shaking off the excess. Deep-fry for 2–3 minutes until golden brown, then drain the tempura and transfer to a tray lined with kitchen paper. Season with salt and pepper. Keep warm.

To serve
Arrange the smoked salmon on four chilled plates and top with a quenelle of crab, a cauliflower tempura and a teaspoon of avocado purée.

Riesling from Germany, Alsace or Clare Valley, Australia, works well with this dish. A white Bordeaux is equally good, or a Rhône such as a Châteauneuf-du-Pape or a Saint-Joseph.

smoked salmon and mussel cold plate

serves 4

4–8 large slices of smoked salmon
2–3 dozen mussels, cooked or smoked
4 tablespoons tomato concassé (see p. 136)
1 teaspoon small capers, chopped
2 teaspoons parsley, shredded
1 teaspoon mint leaves, chopped
black pepper, freshly ground
dillisk (dulse) or sea vegetable of your choice

dressing
2 tablespoons virgin olive oil
1 teaspoon white wine vinegar
1 teaspoon mustard

Place the dressing ingredients in a screw-topped jar. Shake the contents well until you have a nice thick emulsion.

Arrange smoked salmon on four dinner plates and scatter the mussels on top.

Spread tomato concassé over and sprinkle with capers, parsley and mint.

Dust with a little black pepper and add a dash of the dressing.

Garnish with strands of dillisk or sea vegetable of your choice.

Riesling, Sipp Mack, Alsace, France. The French home of Riesling is Alsace, and the crisp acidity, coupled with stone fruit, will boost the mussels and sea vegetable as well as the salmon.

smoked salmon dauphinoise

serves 4

110 g / 4 oz hot-smoked salmon, chopped
110 g / 4 oz cold-smoked salmon, chopped
450 g / 1 lb floury potatoes, thinly sliced
300 ml / ½ pint cream (or use half milk, half cream)
1–2 cloves garlic, crushed
salt and black pepper
50 g / 2 oz Cheddar cheese, grated (optional)

Preheat the oven to 200 °C / 400 °F / Gas mark 6.

Place the cream (and milk if using), potato slices and seasoning in a large saucepan and slowly bring to boiling point over a low heat. Simmer for almost 15 minutes, mixing gently to ensure potatoes cook evenly. When almost, but not fully, cooked and the mixture is nice and creamy, place half into a large greased ovenproof dish. Scatter the chopped smoked salmon over the mixture and cover with the remaining potato and cream mix.

If you wish, top with grated cheese before baking. This will give the dish more substance.

Bake for 30–40 minutes until the top is nice and golden.

Serve with a crisp green salad.

Riesling, Kabinett Trocken, Schumacher, Rheingau, Germany. The 'trocken' (dry) element is the key to its clean mineral flavour. Elegance personified in this classic dish and wine.

salmon in social history and tradition

The Céide Fields in County Mayo are the oldest known field systems in the world. When the first settlers arrived in the north-west of Ireland almost six millennia ago, it is likely that they found rivers and streams with well-established salmon stocks that had arrived four to six millennia earlier. It is not surprising then, that the salmon has been marvelled at and remarked upon by scribes and writers in Ireland from the earliest times.

Salmon is deeply embedded in our mythology and folklore, and the legends surrounding it have been told and re-told down the millennia. One such legend, the Salmon of Knowledge, tells the story of the ancient Irish warrior Fionn Mac Cumhail and how, as a boy, he met the leprechaun-like druid and poet Finnegas near the River Boyne and went to study under him. Finnegas had spent seven years trying to catch the 'salmon of knowledge', which lived in a pool on the Boyne. Legend had it that whoever ate the salmon would gain all the knowledge in the world. Eventually, Finnegas caught the fish and told the young Fionn to cook it for him. While cooking it, Fionn burnt his thumb and instinctively put it in his mouth, swallowing a piece of the salmon's skin. This imbued him with all the salmon's wisdom. As a grown man, he knew instantly how to vanquish his enemies, and in other legends he often calls on the salmon's knowledge by sucking his thumb.

Christianity gradually took over from the druidic traditions following the arrival of St Patrick around 450 AD, and through a mixture of meditation and asceticism idealistic young men were drawn to a life of prayer and penance. One of these, Manchán, who was one of Patrick's own converts, became a recluse and a hermit. As was the case with St Kevin in Glendalough, disciples gathered around this holy man, and reluctantly he became the head of a small group of monks. Finding himself and his followers dependent on nature and the good will of others, he is said to have penned the poem known as 'St Manchán's Prayer', and in one stanza makes specific mention of the importance of salmon and trout as a food source for the community.

> And all I ask for housekeeping
> I get and pay no fees,
> Leeks from the garden, poultry, game,
> Salmon and trout and bees.

Over time, such small religious communities banded together and formed larger monasteries. Invariably these were located near water and took advantage of the free and abundant protein to be found in the larger salmon rivers. As the monasteries grew, so did their overheads, and so these religious centres also developed into centres of trade for the local area. Salmon was a seasonally valuable commodity and it was not long before salmon and salmon fishing were bartered and traded.

Traditionally, fishing rights were free to those living along the banks of both rivers and lakes in Ireland. The rights of private property gradually encroached upon and ultimately criminalised the traditional customs of common ownership, so that by the turn of the twentieth century salmon fisheries were seen as they are today, primarily as a heritable and valuable private possession.

harvesting salmon

Salmon have been harvested in Ireland since humans first arrived on the north-west coast almost 6,000 years ago. The fish arrived from the sea in pulses and provided highly prized food on a seasonal basis in spring, summer and autumn. It is little wonder that ingenious methods of capturing salmon have been part of the Irish heritage and the Irish countryside for millennia. Originally various forms of stone enclosures were used, and the remnants of these are to be seen to this day on the shores of Strangford Lough near Killyleagh, Co. Down, and at the mouth of the Doonbeg River, Co. Clare. Until recently such salmon boxes or traps were still in use to harvest salmon commercially on the weirs on the River Moy in Ballina and the River Corrib in Galway.

In addition to traps, Ireland also boasts a wide range of salmon nets around the coast. In many locations, during the summer months, the draft-net fishermen can be seen waiting patiently on the shore, their net neatly folded in the back of the boat.

Traditional drift netting took place further out at sea and involved the release of a wall of 800–1,600 metres of floating netting behind a small trawler, a so called half-decker, or a large currach. Eventually, the closure of the offshore salmon fishery, on conservation grounds, saw the end of drift net fishing in 2007.

Other commercial salmon fisheries in Ireland included the coastal bag-net fishery, comprising a series of vertical poles on which is strung a large box-shaped net which includes a series of passageways and narrow pockets leading in to the bunt of the net.

Along the Barrow, Nore and Suir, the 'Three Sisters' which flow into Waterford Harbour, there is a tradition of using a pair of long, narrow river boats called cots in combination with a unique technique known as snap netting. The net is strung out between the cots and the boats are allowed to drift downstream in the estuary. Once a salmon hits the net, it is snapped shut between the boats and the prize is hauled aboard.

Rod and line fishing, in one form or another, has been practised in Ireland for millennia, but it was in the late eighteenth and early nineteenth century that angling as a hobby or sport became popular. Despite the fact that it was a sport, the harvest was retained and either used by the local household or sold on.

Angling was traditionally very much part of life for locals and landowners on the large eastern rivers. In the west, sport fishing for salmon and sea trout did not become an important pursuit until the arrival of the country house and country-house sporting parties in the nineteenth century. The value of the fisheries in terms of employment of ghillies and staff required for the upkeep of the large houses became a significant part of the rural economy. It was not so much the fish flesh as the pursuit of the salmon which provided the income. Yet it was in these houses that the now traditional methods of cooking and smoking salmon were first developed and refined. In this book we have fine examples of several of these traditional recipes, often including the best of local ingredients, such as Irish whiskey, and native tree species, such as oak, for the smoking of the salmon. KW

dinners & special occasions

orange-glazed salmon fillets with mango salsa

serves 4

4 salmon fillets, 175 g / 6 oz each,
with skin
1 tablespoon chilli powder
450 ml / 16 fl oz orange juice,
freshly squeezed
110 ml / 4 fl oz Cointreau
1 tablespoon olive oil
½ orange
sea salt to season

mango salsa
1 ripe mango, peeled, stoned
and finely diced
1 small red onion, finely diced
½ red bell pepper, finely diced
½ orange or yellow bell pepper,
finely diced
3 tablespoons coriander,
chopped
2 tablespoons extra-virgin
olive oil

Combine all the mango salsa ingredients in a bowl. Chill for a minimum of 1 hour before serving.

Slice the ½ orange into thin slices, halve the slices and place on a pan with a little oil.

Fry until golden. Take off the heat and leave aside.

Season the flesh side of the salmon fillets with chilli powder and sea salt.

In a saucepan, combine orange juice and Cointreau and reduce (see p. 12) by three-quarters to approximately 110 ml / 4 fl oz.

Heat the oil on a hot pan. Add the salmon fillets, flesh side down, and cook over medium heat for 3–4 minutes. Turn fillets over and cook for a further 3–4 minutes.

Add the reduced juice for the last minute of cooking.

Remove salmon and sauce to serving plates and top with caramelised orange slices. Serve mango salsa on the side.

Sauvignon Blanc, Greywacke, Marlborough, New Zealand. This mouth-watering wine has a perfumed blossom-like aroma. Nice with mango tastes. A certain delicious flintiness on the palate will cut the oil in the fish and lead you on to a nice lingering citrus finish.

Photography Barry McCall

fillet of wild salmon, tandoori gnocchi, sorrel sauce

serves 4

4 salmon fillets, 175 g / 6 oz each,
with skin
15 g / ½ oz butter
fine salt
Maldon salt crystals

gnocchi
500 g / 18 oz potatoes
110 g / 4 oz '00' pasta flour
50 g / 2 oz Parmesan, finely grated
15 g / ½ oz melted butter
1 teaspoon tandoori spice
1 egg

sorrel sauce
200 ml / 7 fl oz fish stock
(see p. 130)
50 g / 2 oz sorrel leaves
200 g / 7 oz Bordier butter
3–4 drops lemon juice

butter emulsion
50 g / 2 oz butter
50 ml / 2 fl oz stock or water

finishing requirements
tandoori spice
selection of fresh, soft herbs

Gnocchi
Preheat oven to 180 °C / 350 °F / Gas mark 4.
Bake the potatoes on a bed of rock salt for 40 minutes.
Pass through a potato ricer into a bowl and mix in the remainder of the ingredients while the potato is still warm.
Shape into 15 g / ½ oz gnocchi using a gnocchi paddle and blanch in simmering salted water for 2½ minutes.
The gnocchi will float when cooked.
Refresh in iced water and reserve until needed.

Sauce
Place the fish stock in a pan and reduce by half (see p. 12).
Add the sorrel leaves, remove from the heat and leave to sit for 2–3 minutes.
Pass the stock through a chinois into a clean pan.
Heat and whisk in the butter a little at a time.
Adjust the seasoning with lemon juice and salt.
Keep warm until required.

Salmon
Lightly season the salmon fillets with fine salt and place in a vacuum bag with a small knob of butter.
Cook in a water bath preheated to 56 °C / 132.8 °F for 12 minutes.
When cooked, remove and rest for 3 minutes.
On a clean board, carefully peel off the skin and scrape away the bloodline with a paring knife.
Season the top side with the Maldon salt crystals and keep warm.

Butter emulsion
Heat stock or water in a pan and whisk in a knob of butter until melted and emulsified.

Assembly and plating up (per portion)
Warm the gnocchi in the butter emulsion with a pinch of tandoori spice.

Flash the salmon under the salamander or grill for 30 seconds to boost the temperature. Place the salmon in the centre of the plate and arrange 3–4 gnocchi on top.

With a handheld blender, buzz the sorrel sauce and spoon over.
Garnish with fresh herbs.

Riesling, Egon Müller, Scharzhofberger, Mosel, Germany. Mellow mineral and tangy lime, softened by flowers and honey, will add to all three elements of this recipe.

salmon cutlet with honey and mustard sauce and roasted vegetables

serves 4

4 salmon cutlets, 175 g / 6 oz each
salt and pepper

1 aubergine, sliced lengthways
2 onions, sliced
3 large tomatoes, halved
175 g / 6 oz flat mushrooms
olive oil
salt
black pepper, freshly ground

sauce
300 ml / ½ pint cream
1 tablespoon wholegrain mustard
2 teaspoons Dijon mustard
1 tablespoon honey

Preheat the oven to 190 °C / 375 °F / Gas mark 5. Bake the cutlets for 8–10 minutes. Season to taste.

Brush all the vegetables with olive oil, then roast for 7–8 minutes, turning and basting once or twice. Season with salt and black pepper.

Place all the sauce ingredients in a saucepan, whisk together, bring to the boil and simmer gently for 1 minute.

To serve, heat four dinner plates, place a cutlet on each, put the roasted vegetables alongside and drizzle with honey and mustard sauce.

Pinot Grigio Riserva, Mezzacorona, Trentino, Italy. A touch of oak gives this wine extra weight and complexity to handle the mustard sauce and provide a nice balance of flavours with the roasted vegetables.

wild salmon glazed with apple syrup

serves 4

4 wild salmon fillets, 175 g /
6 oz each, with skin
110 ml / 4 fl oz apple cider
25 ml / 1 fl oz apple syrup
(see p. 83)
1 tablespoon rapeseed or
sunflower oil
1 lime, cut into 4 wedges

In a saucepan heat the apple cider and syrup and reduce (see p. 12) until you have a nice syrupy mix.

Pour this syrup over the salmon, flesh side down, cover and leave aside for 10–12 minutes for the flavours to seep into the salmon.

Brush a ridged pan with a little oil and cook the salmon fillets 3–4 minutes on each side until the skin is crisp and the flesh just tender but not too firm.

Serve on a bed of colcannon (see p. 69) and garnish with a lime wedge.

If you really are having wild salmon, why not try a very dry Chardonnay, Mâcon-Uchizy, Domaine Talmard, Mâcon-Villages, France. The flinty, oily taste is well worth experiencing and there is a wonderful long finish which will mingle with the fruity salmon.

Chef **Vivian Kelly** *Kieran's Kitchen, Roadside Tavern* **Burren Smokehouse** *Lisdoonvarna, Co. Clare* burrensmokehouse.ie

EURO-TOQUES

Burren hot-smoked organic salmon on a bed of colcannon with stir-fry vegetables

serves 4

700 g / 1 ½ lb Burren Smokehouse
hot-smoked organic salmon

colcannon
450 g / 1 lb floury potatoes, peeled
1 head cabbage, finely shredded
(4 cups shredded leaves)
2 tablespoons spring onions,
chopped
2 tablespoons butter
50 ml / 2 fl oz milk, heated
salt and black pepper to taste

stir-fry vegetables
1 red pepper
1 onion
1 courgette
8 mushrooms
1 teaspoon soya sauce
1 tablespoon olive oil, for frying

mustard cream sauce
1 tablespoon wholegrain mustard
600 ml / 1 pint cream
2 tablespoons white wine

Colcannon
Boil the potatoes in lightly salted water until tender, then drain. Boil the cabbage for about 5 minutes, drain and set aside. Mash the potatoes with spring onions, butter and milk. Add salt and pepper to taste. Fold in the cabbage.

Stir-fry vegetables
Cut all vegetables in strips and stir-fry in olive oil until they are soft.

Mustard cream sauce
Combine cream, white wine and mustard and bring to the boil. Remove from the heat and keep warm.

Assembly
Preheat the oven to 180 °C / 350 °F / Gas mark 4.
Cut the hot-smoked organic salmon into 4 pieces.
Heat the salmon in the oven for 5 minutes.

To serve, create a base of colcannon, arrange stir-fry vegetables on top and pour the mustard cream sauce over the vegetables.

Top the dish with the hot-smoked salmon.

Why not try one of the Burren Brewery craft beers from the Roadside Tavern if you are near Co. Clare. Otherwise, the old reliables, Guinness and Murphy's, will cut mustard with this hearty dish.

Chef **Amy Caviston** *A. Caviston* *Greystones, Co. Wicklow* acaviston.ie
EURO-TOQUES

Clare Island organic salmon wrapped in banana leaf with fennel, lemon, chilli, lemongrass, white wine and coriander

serves 2

2 salmon darnes,
200 g / 7 oz each, skinned
and pin-boned
2 banana leaves (or baking
parchment or tin foil)
1 fennel bulb, thinly sliced
1 stalk lemongrass, bruised
and chopped
1 chilli, finely sliced
½ lemon, sliced
good handful coriander,
chopped
2 glugs dry white wine
1 teaspoon rapeseed oil

Preheat the oven to 180 °C / 350 °F / Gas mark 4.

In a pan, heat the rapeseed oil and gently sweat the chilli, lemongrass and fennel for about 5 minutes until al dente

Place each salmon darne on to an individual banana leaf (or piece of baking parchment or tin foil).

Place the chilli, lemongrass, fennel, lemon and coriander on top of the salmon.

Wrap as if to make a parcel and add a glug of wine to each, wet the banana leaf around the edges to seal, or fold in the paper/foil tightly.

Place in the oven and cook for 15 minutes.

After removing it from the oven, let it rest for about 5 minutes before serving.

To serve, place the sealed package on the individual plate, leaving your guest to open it and get the waft of flavours. (Warn your guests not to try to eat banana leaf as it is quite fibrous.)

Serve with baby potatoes and fresh green beans or plain rice.

Sauvignon Blanc, Walnut Block, Marlborough, New Zealand. This fruity wine will blend well with all the interesting components of the recipe.

grilled darne of wild salmon with Cornamona smoked salmon and chive cream sauce

serves 4

4 wild salmon darnes, 225 g / 8 oz
each, with skin
½ lemon, juice only
4–6 tablespoons rapeseed oil
salt and coarsely ground black
pepper
1 lemon, cut into 4 wedges
chives, finely chopped for garnish

sauce

1 shallot, finely chopped
2 tablespoons rapeseed oil
50 ml / 2 fl oz dry white wine
50 ml / 2 fl oz fish stock (see p. 136)
110 ml / 4 fl oz fresh cream
6 chives, finely chopped
110 g / 4 oz Cornamona smoked
salmon, finely diced
black pepper, freshly ground

Sauce

Heat a large pan, add rapeseed oil and sauté the shallots until soft and without colour. Add white wine and reduce slightly. Add fish stock, reduce by half (see p. 12), add cream and bring slowly to the boil.

Simmer for 5–8 minutes until it thickens to a sauce consistency. Add diced smoked salmon and chives and cook for a further 1–2 minutes. Taste and season with pepper.

Salmon darnes

Preheat grill to 190 °C / 375 °F / Gas mark 5. Rub salmon darnes with rapeseed oil and lightly season with salt and crushed black pepper.

Place under grill and cook skin side up for approx. 6 minutes until the skin has become crispy, then turn and cook for a further 3–5 minutes until you start to see the flakes of the salmon separate. Ideally, the grilled salmon should have a lightly seared crust and a nice crispy skin and be medium-rare on the inside. Remove from grill and allow to rest for 5 minutes.

To serve, place a salmon darne on each of four warmed plates, pour smoked salmon sauce over the fish, garnish with freshly cut lemons wedges and chopped chives. Serve with boiled new potatoes and a fresh garden salad.

Fishing on Lough Inagh, Connemara

Sancerre, Domaine des Brosses, Loire, France. Crisp and clean, with ripe gooseberries on the palate. A nice mineral intensity and lime will give zest to the creamy sauce.

pan-seared wild salmon, soy and caper glaze, with smoked salmon and nori arancini

In Italian, 'arancini' means little oranges, the name given to fried rice balls coated in breadcrumbs, as used in this dish.

serves 4

4 salmon fillets, 175 g / 6 oz each
rapeseed oil, for frying
1 cucumber, peeled

soy and caper glaze
1 tablespoon spring onion, chopped
1 tablespoon coriander, chopped
2 tablespoons capers, chopped
1 tablespoon soy sauce
1 teaspoon honey
2 tablespoons sunflower oil
1 teaspoon Dijon mustard

arancini
300 ml / ½ pint fish stock
(see p. 136)
1 tablespoon shallots, diced
1 tablespoon pickled ginger, diced
110 g / 4 oz risotto rice
50 g / 2 oz smoked salmon, diced
2 sheets Nori seaweed, soaked and chopped
1 tablespoon dill, chopped
300 g / 11 oz breadcrumbs

lemon and saffron mayonnaise
1 lemon, zest and juice
25 g / 1 oz palm sugar
pinch saffron strands
4 egg yolks
400 ml / 14 fl oz olive or rapeseed oil

pea purée
200 g / 7 oz peas
110 g / 4 oz spinach
6 leaves mint
salt

Soy and caper glaze
Combine all ingredients to make a paste.

Arancini
Place risotto rice with shallots, ginger and seaweed in a heavy-based wide saucepan over medium heat. Add a ladle of fish stock. Turn up the heat and keep stirring and adding stock, one ladle at a time, until you have a nice creamy consistency. Add the smoked salmon. Leave to cool. Roll the risotto into 8 ball shapes and breadcrumb them.

Pea purée
Boil the peas in salty boiling water until soft. Turn off the heat and add in spinach and mint. After 1 minute, drain, then purée in a food processor. Pass through a fine sieve.

Lemon and saffron mayonnaise
Put the egg yolks in a food processor, spin the blade, then add in the lemon zest and juice, palm sugar and saffron. Add the oil slowly until it reaches mayonnaise texture.

Salmon
Preheat the oven to 170 °C / 325 °F / Gas mark 3.
Sear the salmon fillets in a hot pan coated with a little rapeseed oil. Transfer to a tray and coat each fillet with a topping of glaze. Bake in the oven for 10 minutes.

Finishing and assembly
Deep-fry the arancini. Shave the cucumber to garnish.
To serve, place a glazed salmon fillet on each of four warmed plates, sprinkle with cucumber shavings, place two arancini next to the salmon and serve lemon and saffron mayonnaise in accompanying bowls.

Ballynahinch Fishing Record (1926–1962). Page illustrating His Highness The Maharaja Ranjitsinhji's catch of a 5 lb 5 oz salmon on 23rd August 1927.

Saint-Véran 'En Crêches', Domaine Saumaize, Burgundy, 2010. This white is fruity and not too dry, providing a good balance with this complex dish.

poached wild salmon with Irish butter sauce

For maximum flavour, we cook the wild salmon in the time-honoured way, by poaching it gently in well-salted boiling water. Better still, use sea water if you are close to the coast.

serves 8

1.1 kg / 2½ lb fresh Irish wild salmon, centre cut
water
salt

Irish butter sauce
2 egg yolks
1 dessertspoon cold water
110 g / 4 oz butter, diced
1 teaspoon lemon juice

garnish
sprigs of flat parsley or watercress

If not using sea water, it is important to get the proportion of salt to water right. We use one rounded tablespoon of salt to every 1.2 litres / 40 fl oz of water.

Although the fish or piece of fish should be just covered with water, the aim is to use the minimum amount of water to preserve the maximum flavour; therefore, one should use a saucepan that will fit the fish exactly. An oval cast-iron saucepan is usually perfect.

Half fill the pan with salted water and bring to the boil. Put in the piece of fish, just covering with water, and bring back to the boil. Simmer gently for 20 minutes.

Turn off the heat, allow the fish to sit in the water. Serve within 15–20 minutes.

Meanwhile make the Irish butter sauce. Put the egg yolks into a heavy-bottomed stainless-steel saucepan on a very low heat. Add the cold water and whisk thoroughly.

Add the butter bit by bit, whisking all the time. As soon as one piece melts, add the next. The mixture will gradually thicken, but if it shows signs of becoming too thick or 'scrambling' slightly, remove from the heat immediately and add a little cold water if necessary. Do not leave the pan or stop whisking until the sauce is made. Finally, add the lemon juice to taste. Pour into a bowl and keep warm over hot, but not boiling, water.

To serve, lift the cooked salmon carefully from the poaching liquid.

Peel off the skin gently. Garnish with sprigs of parsley or watercress.

Serve with the Irish butter sauce.

Chardonnay, 'Milmanda', Conca de Barbera, Spain. Slightly creamy, with apricot tastes, a lovely combination from an unusual source. A nice match for this simply classic dish.

Photography Kevin Thornton

smoked wild Irish salmon with cucumber jelly and beluga caviar

This recipe includes the method we use at Thornton's for marinating and smoking the wild salmon we get during the relatively short salmon season. We use only wild fish at Thornton's. Not everyone will want to go to the trouble of smoking salmon at home, but I wanted to show how we do it at the restaurant. Smoked salmon is a firm favorite during the festive season and this recipe is a great light starter. The caviar element is optional. This recipe is for four persons; however, I suggest you marinate a larger fillet of salmon, which will last for seven days in a well-cooled refrigerator and is always a great stand-by.

serves 4

1.25 kg / 2 lb 12 oz wild Atlantic
salmon fillet, with skin
1 kg / 2 lb 4 oz rock salt
500 g / 18 oz granulated sugar
250 g / 9 oz crushed black pepper
1 small bunch fresh dill
1 small bunch fennel fronds
1 tablespoon virgin olive oil

cucumber jelly
1 organic cucumber, peeled,
de-seeded and roughly chopped
5 g / ¼ oz carrageen moss (instead
of gelatin)
5 g / ¼ oz salmon roe
25 ml / 1 fl oz fish stock (see p. 136)
½ organic cucumber, peeled,
de-seeded and finely diced
1 tablespoon sea salt
freshly ground white pepper

lemon and dill vinaigrette
1 unwaxed lemon, zest and juice
110 ml / 4 fl oz cider vinegar
25 ml / 1 fl oz spring water
400 ml / 14 fl oz olive oil
50 ml / 2 fl oz grapefruit juice
white pepper, freshly ground
sea salt
1 sprig fresh dill, chopped

potato garnish
2–3 medium potatoes, peeled
(Maris Piper)
1 litre sunflower oil
sea salt
lemon oil (lemon zest and virgin
olive oil mixed)

caviar and cucumber garnish
110 g / 4 oz beluga caviar
110 g / 4 oz salmon roe
1 lemon, zest
20 little balls of cucumber
(made using a selfrino shaper)

Marinade and smoking
Remove the pin bones from the salmon. Mix the salt, sugar and black pepper together. Place half the salt mixture in a deep dish and lay the salmon on it. Place the dill and fennel over the salmon, then completely cover the salmon with the remainder of the salt mixture. Cover the dish with a linen cloth and refrigerate at 2 °C / 35 °F for 14–16 hours (If you are doing this at home, your fridge will be set at approx. 6 °C / 43 °F, so leave the salmon in overnight until it is firm but not overly firm.)

Remove the salmon from the salt mixture and wash by placing the salmon in a stainless steel bowl and allowing cold water to run on it for 15 minutes. Dry the salmon by wrapping it in a muslin cloth or clean tea towel.

Hang the salmon in the smoking room at 32 °C / 90 °F for 5 days. The salmon should have a slight brown tint once it is sufficiently smoked. The salmon will last for a couple of weeks in a fridge at 2 °C. Once smoked, remove the outer skin from the salmon.

Cucumber jelly
Juice the chopped cucumber in a juicer. Remove and strain through a fine sieve. Heat the stock in a stainless steel pot and add the carrageen moss. Cook over a medium heat for two minutes. Remove and strain into the cucumber juice, add the diced cucumber and salmon roe to the cucumber juice, taste for seasoning and correct by adding salt and pepper. Pour the juice into a deep stainless steel tray and refrigerate until set. Remove from the fridge and cut the jelly into circular shapes using a 5 mm / ¼ inch pastry cutter.

Lemon and dill vinaigrette
Chop and blanch the lemon zest, refresh, and place in a stainless steel bowl. Whisk in the lemon juice, cider vinegar and olive oil. Add the grapefruit juice and spring water, season with the salt and pepper. Taste and correct the seasoning if necessary. Add the chopped dill at the last moment.

Potato garnish
Preheat deep-fat fryer with sunflower oil to reach 180 °C / 350 °F. Slice the potato very thinly and cut into 20 triangles. Fry the triangles until golden brown. Remove and place on kitchen paper, season with sea salt.

Assembly
Slice the salmon very thinly, about 75 g / 3 oz per portion. Place the cucumber jelly in the centre of the plate and arrange the salmon on top. Arrange the caviar and cucumber garnish around the plate. Sprinkle a little lemon and dill vinaigrette on the salmon and around the plate. Insert the tips of the potato triangles in the cucumber jelly and sprinkle with lemon oil. Serve.

Chablis, Premier Cru, 'Fourchaume', Domaine Denis Race, France, 2011.

Ummera smoked salmon with boxty potato cake, rocket and horseradish crème fraiche

Ummera Smokehouse, nestled in the Argideen Valley near Timoleague in West Cork, has been smoking salmon since the 1970s: wild Atlantic salmon initially, and for the last 10 years sustainably grown organic salmon from the west coast.

Anthony Creswell of Ummera is a firm believer that his smoked salmon should be enjoyed as it is, without any further embellishment, but John Finn of the fabulous Finn's Table restaurant in Kinsale has come up with this recipe, of which even Anthony approves!

serves 6

600 g / 1 lb 5 oz Ummera smoked organic salmon, thinly sliced

boxty potato cake
150 g / 5 oz potato, mashed
150 g / 5 oz raw potato, grated
1 egg
½ lemon, zest
110 g / 4 oz flour
50 ml / 2 fl oz buttermilk

horseradish sauce
150 ml / 5 fl oz crème fraiche
25 g / 1 oz fresh horseradish, grated
½ lemon, zest
1 tablespoon olive oil
sea salt and black pepper

rocket leaves to garnish

Mix the mashed potato and grated potato, add the egg, buttermilk and lemon zest; finally, add the flour and mix well.

Shape the mixture into 6 balls and flatten.

Heat a frying pan and fry the potato cakes on both sides until crispy on a low heat.

Make the horseradish sauce by combining the ingredients and season to taste with salt and pepper.

To serve, fan smoked salmon slices on the plate, arrange a potato cake on top, place rocket on top again, and pour the sauce around.

A nice glass of dry Stonewell Cider from Co. Cork would complement this perfectly.

pan-seared salmon, vegetable Provençale, saffron mussels, baked beetroot and parsnip chips

serves 6–8

4 salmon fillets, 150 g / 5 oz each,
with skin and pin-boned
pinch salt and black pepper
1 teaspoon lemon juice
olive oil, for frying

basil and vegetable Provençale
50 g / 2 oz courgette, diced
50 g / 2 oz aubergine, diced
50 g / 2 oz fresh tomato, diced
50 g / 2 oz onion, diced
50 g / 2 oz red pepper, diced
25 g / 1 oz tomato purée
1 clove garlic, chopped
olive oil, for frying
110 ml / 4 fl oz white wine
4 large basil leaves
salt and pepper

yellow pepper cream
2 yellow peppers, diced
1 small onion, diced
25 g / 1 oz leek, chopped
1 celery stick, chopped
1 clove garlic, chopped
1 sprig thyme, de-stemmed
200 ml / 7 fl oz double cream
2 tablespoons olive oil
salt and pepper

baked beetroot
1 whole beetroot, peeled
1 tablespoon balsamic vinegar
1 tablespoon olive oil
1 teaspoon brown sugar

parsnip chips
1 parsnip, peeled
sunflower oil, for deep-fat frying
salt

saffron mussels
12 mussels, washed and
de-bearded
25 g / 1 oz onion, diced
1 pinch saffron
25 g / 1 oz butter
200 ml / 7 fl oz white wine
200 ml / 7 fl oz double cream
1 clove garlic, chopped

garnish
1 bunch whole flat-leaf parsley

Basil and vegetable Provençale

Heat oil in a pan, add garlic, tomato and vegetables and cook for 2 minutes.
Add tomato purée and white wine and cook for a further 1–2 minutes. Add basil
and season with salt and pepper. Keep warm.

Salmon

Preheat the oven to 190 °C / 375 °F / Gas mark 5. Season salmon fillets with a little
salt, black pepper and lemon juice. Heat olive oil in a non-stick pan and cook fish, skin
side down, for 2 minutes. Transfer salmon to oven and cook for a further 5 minutes.

Yellow pepper cream

Heat oil in a pan and, over moderate heat, add vegetables, garlic and thyme. Cook
until soft. Season, add cream and simmer for 2 minutes. Blend in a processor and
pass through a fine sieve. Keep warm.

Baked beetroot

Preheat the oven to 190 °C / 375 °F / Gas mark 5. Cook beetroot in salted water
for 20 minutes. Cut beetroot into thin slices. Pan-fry in olive oil for 2 minutes.
Add vinegar and sprinkling of sugar and place in the oven for 4 minutes.

Parsnip chips

Peel the outer skin off the parsnip and, using a vegetable peeler, shave the parsnip
into strips. Deep-fry until golden brown and crisp. Drain on kitchen paper, season
with salt to taste.

Saffron mussels

Put the mussels in a pot with onion, half the wine, the parsley and garlic. Cook until
mussels open. If mussels do not open, discard. Remove mussel flesh from shells.
Add the remaining wine, cream and saffron to the juice in which the mussels cooked
and reduce by half (see p. 12). Whisk in the butter. Add mussel flesh and keep warm.

To serve

Place a round mould in the centre of a plate and fill with the vegetable Provençale.
Place mussels beside the vegetables. Pour yellow pepper cream around the base
of the plate with baked beetroot to the side.

Remove mould and place fish on top of vegetables, topping with parsnip crisps.
Garnish with whole flat-leaf parsley.

Chablis, Domaine Pinson, Burgundy, France. Stony fruit and a nice long mineral finish from this
mid-range-priced wine will combine beautifully with the details in this dish.

salmon with watercress and peach salsa

serves 4

4 salmon fillets, 175 g / 6 oz each, with skin
1 tablespoon mixed peppercorns, crushed
16 new baby potatoes
2 bunches of fresh watercress

peach salsa
2 ripe peaches, peeled, stoned and finely diced
3 spring onions, finely chopped
3 tablespoons coriander, chopped
2 tablespoons lemon juice
2 tablespoons extra-virgin olive oil
dash Tabasco

Combine all the peach salsa ingredients in a bowl. Chill for a minimum of 1 hour before serving.

Boil the baby potatoes in salted water. When boiled, coat in melted butter and keep warm.

Press the crushed peppercorns into the salmon flesh. Oil a hot ridged pan and cook the salmon fillets, skin side down, for 3–4 minutes, then turn over and cook for a further 2–3 minutes until the salmon is firm to the touch.

On four warm dinner plates, arrange the cooked potatoes with salmon on top and garnish with watercress. Place the peach salsa on the side and serve at once.

Furmint, Mézes Mály, Royal Tokaji Wine Company, Hungary. This wine is something different. Its honey and peach notes may seem an unlikely pairing for such a fruity dish, but this rich, smooth wine is essentially dry.

Ní bheathaíonn na briathra na bráithre

Mere words do not feed the friars

hazelnut-crusted salmon

serves 4

4 salmon fillets, 175 g / 6 oz each, with skin
1 tablespoon toasted hazelnuts, crushed
1 tablespoon honey
1 tablespoon Dijon mustard
1 tablespoon flat leaf parsley, chopped
1 teaspoon black peppercorns, crushed
pinch sea salt

Preheat the grill to high.

Grind the hazelnuts, pepper, salt and parsley to make a nice green mix, bind with honey and mustard and press into the salmon flesh.

Place the fish skin side down on a foil-lined grill pan.

Grill for about 8 minutes until the top is caramelised and the fish is firm to the touch.

Verdejo, José Pariente, Rueda, Spain. A wine that will work with this dish of varied tastes. It is full-flavoured, with enough acidity to suit the nutty salmon as well as the tangy, fruity side dishes.

hot-smoked salmon saffron risotto

Risotto is an Italian dish made primarily by stirring stock and often wine into rice that has been sautéed in butter and/or olive oil. The stock is added slowly and the rice must be stirred as it cooks to ensure a creamy texture. Arborio, Vialone Nano and Carnaroli are suitable varieties for this dish. The rice has large grains and takes up to 20 minutes to cook.

serves 4

225 g / 8 oz hot-smoked salmon chunks
2 tablespoons olive oil
25 g / 1 oz butter
4 medium leeks, finely chopped (use only white parts)
350 g / 12 oz risotto rice
300 ml / ½ pint white wine
850 ml / 1½ pint fish stock (see p. 136), simmering
4 tablespoons Parmesan cheese, freshly grated
½ teaspoon saffron threads
1 lemon, zested
1 lemon, cut in wedges
salt and ground white pepper

Put fish stock and saffron threads in a saucepan and put on a low heat to simmer gently.

Melt butter and olive oil in a heavy-based wide saucepan over a medium heat, add the chopped leeks and sauté until tender. Do not colour them.

Add in the rice, stirring for about 2–3 minutes until well coated with the oil and butter. Pour in the wine stir until it all evaporates. Add a ladle of hot fish stock. Turn up the heat and keep stirring and adding stock, one ladle at a time, until you have a nice creamy consistency. The rice should be al dente.

Off the heat, add lemon zest and grated Parmesan, stir, cover the saucepan and leave for 3 minutes.

Fold in the hot-smoked salmon chunks, mix and check for seasoning.

Serve immediately in warm bowls with lemon wedges on the side.

Chenin Blanc, 'Les Argiles', Domaine François Chidaine, Vouvray, Loire, France. A very fine wine. Honey and mineral flavours ensure it is well worth the extra cost in order to do justice to the risotto.

organic Irish salmon, pickled purple cauliflower, soy caramel, horseradish cream

serves 12

750 g / 1 lb 10 oz organic salmon
110 g / 4 oz micro herbs or
baby leaves

brine
200 g / 7 oz sugar
200 g / 7 oz salt
1 litre / 1¾ pint water

soy caramel
200 g / 7 oz caster sugar
110 ml / 4 fl oz water
15 ml / ½ fl oz thick soy sauce

pickled purple cauliflower
½ purple cauliflower head
200 ml / 7 fl oz water
110 g / 4 oz caster sugar
200 ml / 7 fl oz white wine vinegar
pinch salt

horseradish cream
200 ml / 7 fl oz full cream
2 tablespoons horseradish,
freshly grated
salt and pepper

Salmon
Make a brine by placing the salt, sugar and water in a saucepan. Gently heat to dissolve the sugar and salt, then let the brine cool completely. Pin-bone the salmon, remove skin and fat and cut the salmon in strips 5 cm / 2 inches long. Place the salmon in brine for 1 hour. Preheat a water bath to 40 °C / 104 °F. Remove the salmon from the brine and wash it under cold water. Cut the salmon into small cubes and put into a clean vacuum or ziplock bag and seal. Cook the salmon in the bag in preheated water bath for 10 minutes. Remove from the water bath and, leaving the salmon in the bag, cool the salmon completely in iced water. Keep refrigerated in the bag until ready to use.

Soy caramel
Heat the water and sugar until you get a syrup consistency, then cool and mix in the soya sauce.

Pickled purple cauliflower
Bring water, caster sugar, white wine vinegar and salt to boil in a saucepan. Cut cauliflower into very small florets, pour the pickle over the florets and leave to pickle for twelve hours.

Horseradish cream
Put the cream, horseradish and salt and pepper to taste into a food processor and mix on high speed for 3 minutes.

To serve
Using a silicone pastry brush, swipe the soy caramel across the plate, place the salmon in the centre of the plate and scatter cauliflower florets beside the salmon. Put horseradish cream into a squeezy bottle and squeeze dots around the plate. Do the same with the soy caramel. Finally, scatter micro herbs or baby leaves over the plate.

Champagne Gobillard Premier Cru, Grand Reserve, France. This pale gold champagne, flowery with subtle spices, is well respected and good value in the mid-price range.

salmon with spinach and saffron sauce

serves 4

4 salmon fillets, 175 g / 6 oz each
8 spinach leaves, blanched
15 g / ½ oz butter, melted
salt and black pepper

sauce
125 ml / 4 fl oz very hot fish stock
(see p. 136)
1–2 strands saffron
1 tablespoon lemon juice
3 egg yolks, well-beaten
75 ml / 3 fl oz cream
25 g / 1 oz butter, cubed
salt and pepper to season

Grease an ovenproof dish. Blanch the spinach leaves by dipping first in boiling water, then in cold, and finally patting dry with a clean kitchen towel.
Spread four leaves on bottom of greased dish and brush with melted butter.
Place a salmon fillet in the centre of each leaf and sprinkle with salt and pepper.
Cover with remaining spinach leaves and brush with melted butter.
Steam for 10–12 minutes or microwave for 4–5 minutes.

Sauce
Soak the saffron threads in the fish stock and leave to infuse for about 20 minutes. Strain the stock and discard the threads. Heat the saffron-flavoured fish stock and when hot, pour over the egg yolks, whisking well. Add lemon juice and cream, and whisk again. Now add the butter, cube by cube, stirring and re-heating until the sauce is thick and glossy.

Pour the hot sauce on the warmed dinner plates and place the fish on top.
Serve with steamed baby carrots and baby potatoes tossed in melted butter.

Viognier is the perfect grape match. Try south of France, California or Australia. Clay Station from California is a good choice. A lovely honeysuckle nose followed up with a luscious fruit character balanced by a crisp acidity on the palate.

pan-seared salmon with shallot sauce

serves 4

4 salmon fillets, 175 g / 6 oz each,
4 tablespoons shallots, finely
chopped
4 tablespoons white wine vinegar
225 g / 8 oz cubes of unsalted
butter
2 tablespoons water
16–18 new potatoes, scrubbed
clean, skin left on
sunflower oil
1 tablespoon chopped chives
salt and pepper

Place the shallots, vinegar and water in a saucepan, bring to the boil and reduce by half (see p. 12).
Whisk the butter cubes in one by one, whisking all the time and keeping off the heat every now and then. Season and keep warm.
Cook the new potatoes until tender, drain and keep warm with a cloth over them.
Brush the salmon with oil and season with salt and pepper.
Heat a pan until very hot, oil lightly, place the salmon skin side down, leave for 3–4 minutes without touching, then turn over and cook for 1–2 minutes until firm to the touch.
Transfer to the serving plates, skin side up.
Serve with the shallot sauce, new potatoes and a sprinkling of chives.

If it is for a special occasion, why not splash out on a French Chardonnay such as a Montagny, Premier Cru, Domaine Faiveley, Burgundy. With its fresh floral and mineral scents, it will do justice to this special fish. However, any of the classic Chablis or Sancerres will also for this dish.

Achill Island organic smoked salmon with black pudding and crème fraiche served with warm boxty

When I was growing up in Northern Ireland, boxty was part of our diet and a childhood favourite of mine. The quality of the ingredients is very important to me, so I use Sean Kelly's black pudding from Newport. I have paired the earthiness of the black pudding with the Achill Island organic smoked salmon to create this dish, which can be served as a satisfying starter or as a brunch dish.

serves 4

400 g / 14 oz smoked salmon,
thinly sliced
400 g / 14 oz black pudding
400 g / 14 oz red onion marmalade
110 ml / 4 fl oz crème fraiche
50 g / 2 oz chives, chopped
mixed salad leaves

boxty

225 g / 8 oz raw potato,
freshly grated
225 g / 8 oz cooked potato,
mashed
225 g / 8 oz plain flour
1 teaspoon baking powder
pinch of salt
25 g / 1 oz melted butter
110 ml / 4 fl oz full fat milk

Boxty

Extract as much water as possible from the grated raw potato by squeezing in tea towel. Mix the grated and mashed potato together. Sieve the flour, baking powder and salt together and add the potato mixture with the melted butter.
Knead on a floured surface gently to bring everything together. Pull the dough into four pieces, flatten each into a cake, score the dough into quarters, and cook on an oiled pan over a gentle heat until golden brown on each side.

Fry the black pudding on a medium-high heat for 2 minutes on each side.
Warm the red onion marmalade in a small pan over a low heat.
Add the chopped chives to the crème fraiche and mix.

For each serving, place one boxty cake in the centre of a plate and lay the black pudding on top.

Ruffle slices of the smoked salmon on to the black pudding and place a tablespoon of warmed red onion marmalade on top of the smoked salmon.

Arrange the mixed salad leaves around the boxty and place a dollop of crème fraiche and chive mix on the side.

Malvasi, Bellone, Trebbiano blend, Capolemole Cori Bianco, Lazio, Italy. An organic wine from a single vineyard, this is deliciously light on fruit but has a creamy texture that will soak into the pudding and marmalade. Well worth seeking out.

pan-seared salmon with warm potato and crab salad, lemon aioli and herbs

serves 4

4 salmon fillets, 150 g / 5 oz each, with skin and pin-boned
olive oil, for frying
salt and ground pepper

aioli
2 egg yolks
125 ml / 4½ fl oz rapeseed oil
½ clove garlic, crushed
1 teaspoon cider vinegar
or
1 teaspoon white wine vinegar
½ lemon, juice and zest
salt and pepper

salad
15 baby potatoes, cooked, peeled and diced
25 g / 1 oz shallots, chopped
15 g / ½ oz chives, chopped
15 g / ½ oz parsley, chopped
50 g / 2 oz white crab meat, cooked and picked
1 lemon, zest
1 teaspoon olive oil
salt and pepper
generous bunch of soft herbs such as chives, chervil, dill, parsley (stalks removed)
handful of endive leaves

Aioli
In a blender place the egg yolks and vinegar. Blend slowly till mixed.

Slowly add the oil over approx. 30 seconds; these are the most important moments in making the aioli. When the aioli reaches the consistency you desire add the garlic, lemon juice and zest. Season to taste and chill.

Salad
Heat a non-stick frying pan, add a couple of drops of olive oil. Add the diced potatoes and warm without colouring. Add the chopped shallots and cook for 1 minute.

Add the crab and again warm through. Remove from the heat and add the chopped herbs, lemon zest and seasoning. Keep warm.

Salmon
Preheat the oven to 180 °C / 350 °F / Gas mark 4.
Heat a non-stick frying pan. Drizzle with a little olive oil. Season the fish with fresh ground salt and pepper.

When the oil is hot enough but not smoking, place the fish skin side down in the pan, turn the heat down slightly and cook for 3–4 minutes. Place the pan in the oven and allow to cook for 5–6 minutes.
If you like your fish cooked a little bit more then leave it in the oven a little longer.

Remove the pan from the oven and turn the fish over so the skin side is now up and allow to rest for 2–3 minutes.

To serve, place a mound of the potato and crab salad in the centre of the plate. Place the hot fish on top and place a good dollop of the aioli on the plate.

Garnish the fish with a small salad of the picked herbs and a little endive.

Sauvignon Blanc, Pouilly-Fumé, Bouisson Renard, Loire, France. From a great producer, Didier Daguenau, this wine has the necessary tangy fruit and chalky flavours to blend with both crab and salmon richness.

Photography Walter Pfeiffer

salmon with sweet and sour peppers, olive and basil crushed potatoes

serves 4

4 salmon fillets, 150 g / 5 oz each
olive oil
sea salt
black pepper

sweet and sour peppers
4 red peppers, cored and de-seeded
olive oil
1 teaspoon sugar
splash red wine vinegar
or
balsamic vinegar
salt

crushed potatoes
500 g / 18 oz waxy new
potatoes (Charlotte)
½ lemon, juice
2 teaspoons basil, chopped
2 teaspoons black olives, chopped
2 shallots, finely diced
olive oil
seasoning

Peppers
Cut the peppers into thin slices.

Heat a large frying pan or wok and fry the peppers in olive oil until soft.

Add the sugar and the vinegar and simmer for 1–2 minutes. Turn off the heat and leave until serving.

Potatoes
Boil the potatoes in salted water. When cooked peel off the skin and lightly crush with a fork. Fry the diced shallot in olive oil and cook on a low heat until soft with no colour.

Add the shallots and oil to the potatoes with the lemon juice and the olives, keeping the basil separate to be added just before serving.

Salmon
Preheat the oven to 200 °C / 400 °F / Gas mark 6.
Heat a non-stick frying pan, add a drizzle of olive oil and sear the salmon fillets lightly on all sides until golden.

Transfer to preheated oven and bake for 5–6 minutes.

Before serving, warm the potatoes, adjust the seasoning and add the chopped basil.

Spoon the sweet and sour peppers onto warmed plates.
Top with the salmon and serve the crushed potatoes on the side.

Chardonnay, Montagny, Premier Cru, Domaine Faiveley, Burgundy. Splash out if you are cooking this delicious combination of tastes. You will not want to drown them, so try this unoaked burgundy with its crisp, clean flavours.

beetroot- and orange-cured salmon, beetroot and chestnut slaw, sour cream and crispbreads

serves 10

800 g / 1 lb 12 oz salmon fillet,
with skin, pin-boned

cure
110 g / 4 oz brown sugar
175 g / 6 oz rock salt
2 teaspoons black pepper,
freshly ground
75 ml / 3 fl oz vodka
50 g / 2 oz dill, chopped
2 lemons, zest
2 oranges, zest
600 g /1 lb 5 oz raw beetroot,
freshly grated

beetroot and chestnut slaw
800 g / 1 lb 12 oz raw beetroot,
grated
250 g / 9 oz cooked chestnuts,
coarsely chopped
50 ml / 2 fl oz extra virgin olive oil
1 orange, zest and juice
black pepper, freshly ground

crispbreads
1 loaf of crusty white or
sourdough bread, frozen
200 ml / 7 fl oz extra virgin olive oil
rock salt

sour cream
400 ml / 14 fl oz sour cream
1 teaspoon horseradish,
freshly grated
pinch rock salt
black pepper, freshly ground

garnish
sprigs of fresh dill
1 lemon, zest, finely grated

Salmon cure
Place all the cure ingredients in a bowl and combine. Lay the salmon skin side down on a stainless steel tray.

Pour over the curing mixture and ensure all the salmon is completely covered.

Cover the fish with a layer of cling film and place a heavy weight on top of it.

Refrigerate and allow to cure for 48 hours. Unwrap the salmon, pour and scrap away the curing liquid. Thinly slice the salmon and refrigerate until ready to serve.

Beetroot and chestnut slaw
Combine all ingredients and season to taste. Refrigerate until needed.

Crispbreads
Ensure the bread has been frozen overnight or longer if possible. Remove frozen bread from freezer and using a sharp serrated knife, very thinly carve 40 wafer-thin slices.

Brush a baking tray with olive oil, place bread on the tray and drizzle with olive oil and rock salt.

Crisp the bread in a very hot oven for 5 minutes.

Sour cream
Whisk all the ingredients together and season to taste.

To serve, allow 3 slices of the cured salmon, 1 quenelle of sour cream, 1 tablespoon of slaw and 4 crispbreads per person, garnish with a few sprigs of dill and some lemon zest.

The beetroot and sour cream flavours would go down well with either a Pinot Blanc from the Ehmosers in Wagram, Austria, or a beer of choice.

smoked and barbecued salmon with cured cucumber, horseradish cream and smoked paprika oil

Salmon is a superb fish, lending itself to many culinary dishes and diverse methods of preparation. The life of the salmon is amazing and thankfully we now comprehend the need to preserve and protect this vulnerable fish. The advances in salmon farming techniques and quality enable us to continue to enjoy this fine fish in a sustainable way.

serves 4

200 g / 7 oz smoked salmon, sliced thinly

salmon mousse
50 g / 2 oz barbecued salmon
50 g / 2 oz cream
50 g / 2 oz whipped cream
1 pinch cayenne
1 leaf gelatin
½ teaspoon horseradish paste

cured cucumber
½ cucumber, peeled
1 clove garlic, chopped
1 teaspoon lemon juice
2 tablespoons rock salt

paprika oil
3 tablespoons sunflower oil
2 tablespoons smoked paprika

horseradish cream
500 ml / 18 fl oz cream, whipped
½ teaspoon olive oil
¼ teaspoon lemon juice
horseradish to taste

Salmon mousse
Put the gelatin in a little cold water to soften. While this is happening place the cream in a saucepan and bring to the boil, reduce slightly, add in the barbecued salmon and mix along with the cayenne pepper until it comes back to the boil. Remove from the heat and blend until smooth. Allow to cool and then fold in the whipped cream and horseradish paste.

Smoked salmon roulade
Create four evenly sized rectangles of smoked salmon. Lay out cling film on the worktop and layer the rectangles of smoked salmon on it. Place the mousse in a piping bag and pipe a thick line of mousse along the long edge of the smoked salmon; alternatively you could spread the mousse evenly over the salmon. Take the corners of the cling film and roll the salmon over the mousse to create a sausage. Take the ends of the cling film, roll it tight and tie. Refrigerate until firm and then cut to the desired lengths.

Cured cucumber
Put the cucumber through a mandolin or alternatively use a peeler to make long ribbons, until you reach the seedy centre. Discard this centre. Place the cucumber ribbons in a container and mix with the garlic, lemon juice and rock salt. Leave to marinate for 1 hour and then rinse under cold water. The cucumber should be soft.

Paprika oil
Roast the paprika over a high heat for a few seconds, add in the oil and heat slightly. Remove from the heat and leave overnight to marinate. The paprika will settle to the bottom and oil can be poured off.

Horseradish cream
Fold horseradish, cream, olive oil and lemon juice together and refrigerate. The cream will stiffen with the lemon juice.

Try something different and have a Tio Pepe sherry, which works very well. Alternatively, a glass of good Chablis will fit the bill nicely too.

publican's salmon

This is a very simple and healthy dish that allows the full flavour of the salmon to emerge.

serves 4

4 salmon fillets, 200 g / 7 oz each,
with skin, pin-boned
25 g / 1 oz butter, melted
1 tablespoon sunflower oil
12 mussels,
de-bearded and washed
125 ml / 4 fl oz white wine
1 garlic clove, finely chopped
20 cherry tomatoes
8 basil leaves
salt
black pepper

marinade
shot vodka
dash Tabasco
dash Worcester sauce
pinch sea salt
cracked black pepper
1 teaspoon caster sugar

Mix all the marinade ingredients together.

Place the salmon fillets in a ziplock bag or vacuum pack, pour in the marinade, release as much air as possible from the bag, seal carefully and leave to infuse overnight in the refrigerator.

Next day, remove the salmon from the marinade, pat dry with kitchen towels.

Brush the salmon with melted butter.

On a hot pan, add half the sunflower oil and fry the salmon fillets, flesh side down, for 3 minutes.

Under a very hot grill, cook the salmon, skin side up, until skin begins to crisp.

Mussels
Put mussels in a pot with the wine and garlic. Cook for about 3 minutes until mussels open. Ensure you discard any that do not open.

Remove the shells from 8 of the mussels, leaving four in shell for garnish.

Cut the cherry tomatoes in half and flash fry on a hot pan in a little sunflower oil.

Remove from heat and add basil leaves.

To serve, arrange salmon fillets in centre of plate, arrange mussels around and place tomatoes and basil to the side. Serve with boiled new or baby potatoes.

Sauvignon Blanc, with a hint of Viognier, 'L'Arjolle', Côtes de Thongue, Languedoc, France. Lemon, liquorice and honey flavours may make you imagine you are in the south of France. But you are not. You are in Paddy Coyne's pub in Connemara – lucky you! This is classified as a table wine but it is very flavoursome and well made. Also, it is well priced, so you can order more, unless you move on to Guinness.

salmon cooked in yogurt (Bengali doi maach)

I remember while I was still working back home in India, we used to get Irish smoked salmon, gravlax (cured salmon with dill) and sometimes the whole fish as well. It was extremely popular with our guests. Salmon remains one of my favourite fish. This recipe is a popular fish curry from Calcutta in east India. It is only in the Bengal region that you will find fish and yogurt cooked together. The recipe is very simple and all the ingredients are easily available in any Asian store.

serves 4

4 salmon fillets, 175 g / 6 oz each, skinned and pin-boned
1 teaspoon sunflower oil
salt
coriander leaves for garnish

spice paste
⅓ teaspoon turmeric powder
1½ teaspoons coriander powder
¾ teaspoon cumin powder
1 teaspoon red chilli powder
2 teaspoons ginger, chopped
1 clove garlic, chopped
5 tablespoons water
salt to taste

gravy
4 tablespoons rapeseed oil
2 cloves garlic, chopped
½ teaspoon fenugreek seeds
1 green chilli, finely chopped
5 cm / 2 inch cinnamon stick
5 pods green cardamom
3 cloves
2 medium onions, finely sliced
225 ml / 8 fl oz plain yogurt, whipped
¾ teaspoon sugar
2 tomatoes, chopped
850 ml / 1½ pints water
1 teaspoon salt

fresh beans, blanched
cumin seeds, roasted
salt
fresh coriander leaves

Spice paste
Mix all spice powders with the ginger and garlic and water to make a spice mixture.

Gravy
In a large saucepan, heat the rapeseed oil and add the garlic, fenugreek seeds, green chilli, cinnamon and cardamom.

After 30 seconds, add the cloves.
After 10 seconds, add the onions and fry for about 10 minutes until lightly brown.
Add the spice paste and cook on a low heat for 2 more minutes, stirring continuously.

Add 2 tablespoons of water and cook for 1 minute, add 2 more tablespoons of water and simmer for 10 minutes, so that the onions soften and the spices cook properly.

Turn the heat down very low, add the whipped yogurt and stir continuously for 3 minutes. Add the sugar, tomatoes and remainder of water (depending on thickness of gravy required) and 1 teaspoon of salt. Stir well and keep aside.

Salmon
Using a non-stick frying pan heat the oil until hot, place the salmon skin side down on pan and cook for 3 minutes. Sprinkle some sea salt on flesh side, turn and cook for a further 3 minutes until it is just cooked.

In a medium-hot pan, heat rapeseed oil and sauté blanched beans with roasted cumin seeds and salt to taste.

To serve, select a deep plate and pour a large spoonful of sauce into it, place sautéed beans in the centre and put pan-seared salmon on top.

Garnish with fresh coriander leaves.

A beer of choice or a dry, fruity Riesling will always work. However, a pot of mint tea, hot or iced, would mean that you could feel virtuous but sated.

spicy salmon on samphire with saffron sauce

Marsh samphire (Salicornia europaea), also known as sea asparagus, is widely available along our coastline. It is at its best in July and August. The late great cookery writer Jane Grigson suggested using samphire as a summer delicacy to be enjoyed like asparagus. It has vibrant green stalks and a distinctive crispy and salty taste that complements fish dishes particularly well. Do not use seasoning with this recipe as the samphire and smoked salmon contain enough saltiness.

serves 4

4 salmon fillets, 175 g / 6 oz each, with skin
2 teaspoons coriander seeds
2 teaspoons fennel seeds
2 teaspoons black mustard seeds
sunflower oil, for frying

225 g / 8 oz rock samphire, washed
2 teaspoons olive oil
2 litres / 3½ pints water

sauce
150 ml / ¼ pint fish stock (see p. 136)
100 ml / 3½ fl oz white wine vinegar
2–3 shallots, finely chopped (or chopped chives)
4–5 strands saffron
110 g / 4 oz cubed butter, chilled

4 potatoes, cooked and cubed
1 tablespoon sunflower oil
2 tablespoons butter

Toast or dry-fry the seeds and crush using a mortar and pestle.
Coat the flesh part of the salmon with the crushed seeds.
Cover and set aside in a cool place to allow flavours to be absorbed.

Sauce
Soak the saffron threads in the fish stock and leave to infuse for about 20 minutes. Strain the stock and discard the threads. Place the saffron-flavoured fish stock, vinegar and shallots (or chives) in a saucepan, bring to the boil and reduce by two-thirds (see p. 12).
Remove from the heat and whisk in the chilled butter cubes slowly to get a nice gloss. Keep sauce warm by sitting the saucepan in a bowl of hot water.

Toss the cubed potatoes in a pan with sunflower oil and butter and fry until golden. Keep warm in oven until ready to serve.

Fry the salmon in a little oil in a medium-hot pan, skin side down, until the skin is nicely crisp and golden, 3–4 minutes. Turn salmon fillets over and cook the flesh side for 2 minutes until salmon is firm to the touch.

While salmon is frying, blanch the samphire in boiling water for 2–3 minutes, drain well and toss in olive oil.

To serve, place salmon fillet on bed of samphire on a warm plate, drizzle with saffron sauce and arrange cubed potatoes on the side.

Gewürztraminer, Sipp Mack, Alsace, France. With nuances of rose petal and grapefruit on the nose, plus spice to the finish, this classic wine has enough body and aroma to unite the samphire and spices perfectly.

cured wild salmon, oyster cream, cucumber and marsh samphire

serves 6

cured wild salmon
700 g / 1½ lb centre-cut wild salmon fillet, with skin, pin-boned
75 g / 3 oz salt
75 g / 3 oz sugar
50 g / 2 oz dill, set aside 20 small sprigs to garnish the finished dish
25 ml / 1 fl oz brandy

oyster cream
1½ leaves gelatin
12 rock oysters
1 tablespoon horseradish relish
1 tablespoon crème fraiche
pinch salt
1 lemon, juice

pickled cucumber
2 tablespoons sugar
2 tablespoons white wine vinegar
¼ cucumber, peeled and de-seeded

samphire
110 g / 4 oz marsh samphire, bottom thick stalk removed
2 teaspoons olive oil
2 litres / 3½ pints water

garnish
25 g / 1 oz crème fraiche
bunch watercress, picked and washed
1 teaspoon olive oil

Using a food processor, combine the dill, sugar, salt and brandy and liquidise on full power until smooth and well mixed.

Score the salmon fillet lightly on the skin side only. Using cling film, line a tray or dish just large enough to hold the salmon.

Pour one-third of the dill/brandy mix into the bottom of the tray and place the salmon on top, skin side down. Pour the remaining marinade over the top and mix in well, making sure to cover all the fish. Cover with cling film and leave in the refrigerator for 32 hours.

Then turn the fish over on to the flesh side and marinate for another 16 hours, making sure all the fish is covered, and return to the refrigerator. When the marinade is complete, wash the salmon quickly in cold water, dry with a clean towel and place on a chopping board with the skin side down.

With a sharp knife, remove the skin as if filleting a piece of fish and discard the skin.
Slice into 16 equal-sized thin slices.

Oyster cream
Soak the gelatin in ice-cold water. Open the oysters and remove the meat, making sure to keep the juices. Once opened, check for any broken shell and pass the juices through a fine sieve. Place the oyster juice in a small pan and bring to the boil. Squeeze the water from the gelatin and add to the oyster liquid. Whisk to dissolve.

Place the oysters, the oyster juice with gelatin, the horseradish and crème fraiche in the liquidiser and turn it up to full speed. Blitz for 2 minutes, then remove and season with a pinch of salt and lemon juice, pass through a fine sieve and place in a small piping bag or squeezy bottle and keep in fridge.

Pickled cucumber
Bring the vinegar and sugar to the boil and allow to cool.
Cut the cucumber into small dice or thin slices, salt lightly and leave for 10 minutes.
Wash the cucumber quickly in cold water, then dry and place in the sugar/vinegar mixture.

Bring 2 litres of water to the boil and add the samphire, return to the boil for a couple of minutes, remove the samphire and refresh under cold running water. Drain well and drizzle a little olive oil over it but do not add salt as it is already salty enough.

To serve, squeeze a little of the oyster cream on to each plate. Drain the cucumber and place randomly on the plate, centre the salmon on the plate and scatter the samphire over the salmon. Place a small spoon of crème fraiche to the side and garnish with the reserved sprigs of dill and the watercress leaves dressed with olive oil.

Chardonnay, Château de la Saule, Montagny, Permier Cru, Burgundy, France. Peaches and subtle oak from Alain Roy-Thevenin, a top producer of Montagny, is the soulmate for the creamy oyster base.

whole poached wild Blackwater salmon with hollandaise sauce

We are lucky to have access to wild salmon from our beats on the river Blackwater. We cure wild salmon using a variety of different cures for gravlax; we smoke our own salmon and we also serve salmon carpaccio. This recipe is a favourite and it is traditional, simple and delicious: whole poached wild salmon with hollandaise sauce. I think 'less is more' when cooking wild salmon, and this recipe makes the most of the stunning flavour and texture that is unique to wild salmon.

serves 8–10

3 kg / 6 lb 9 oz whole Blackwater
wild salmon, cleaned and gutted,
head and tail left on
water, enough to cover salmon in
fish kettle
2 tablespoons salt
fresh dill and parsley
lemon wedges for garnish

hollandaise sauce
(see p. 134 and double the
quantities for this dish)

Half fill a fish kettle with cold water and add the salt. Cover and bring water to the boil.

Place the whole salmon in the fish kettle, ensuring that the fish is totally covered by water.

Allow the water to come back to the boil, and simmer with the lid on for 20 minutes.

Take the fish kettle off the heat and leave the salmon in the water for 10 minutes to allow it to settle.

Remove the salmon from the fish kettle very carefully and place on a large serving platter. I like to serve with the skin left on but it can be removed if you wish.

Garnish the fish with fresh dill and parsley and lots of lemon wedges.

We serve the salmon whole on a platter at the table, with bowls of hollandaise sauce.

IMAGE DITTE ISAGER.DK

Chardonnay, Chateau de Chamirey, Mercurey, Burgundy, France. Wild salmon cooked in a fish kettle will soak up the woody, earthy, mineral richness of this wine. Definitely worth the extra few euro.

salmon en croute

serves 6

500 g / 18 oz piece of salmon fillet,
skinned and pin bones removed
110 g / 4 oz baby spinach
150 g / 5 oz cream cheese
salt and pepper
450 g / 1 lb all-butter puff pastry
(thawed if using frozen)
1 egg, beaten

Blend the spinach, cream cheese and seasoning until you get a creamy green purée.

Cut the pastry in two halves and roll each half slightly larger than your salmon fillet. Place one piece of pastry on parchment paper and spread half the spinach mix over it, keeping the edges clean and free.

Place the salmon fillet in the centre of this mix, then spread the other half of the spinach mix over the salmon. Brush the edges of the pastry with the beaten egg.

Lift and carefully place the other pastry half on top of the fish. Press the pastry tightly around the salmon and spinach purée to ensure that you release as much air as possible. Press the edges together firmly, sealing them with the help of the egg wash.

Give a nice edge to the pastry by pressing the edges with a fork or crimp. Decorate the top simply by pressing a teaspoon handle gently into the pastry, working in rows from top to bottom to create little scale shapes all over.

If time allows, refrigerate your dish for about 1 hour to rest the pastry. This chills the butter content and improves your final product.

Preheat the oven to 200 °C / 400 °F / Gas mark 6 and place a large baking sheet in the oven to heat.

Remove your salmon en croute from the fridge and glaze all over with beaten egg.

Now carefully slip your pastry package on its parchment paper on to the hot baking sheet and bake for about 30–40 minutes until golden and the fish is cooked.

To check the salmon, insert a skewer or thin sharp knife into the middle, leave for 3 seconds, then test it against the inside of your wrist: if it is hot, the salmon is cooked.

Remove from the oven and leave to rest for about 5 minutes. Slide the salmon on to a serving platter and take it to the table whole, as salmon en croute makes a stunning centrepiece.

Serve with a large bowl of tossed green salad and a hollandaise sauce (see p. 134).

Sangiovese / Cabernet Sauvignon / Merlot, Montecucco Rosso, Campinuovi, Tuscany, Italy. Why not have a red, the perfect partner for the oven-baked pastry, salmon and cream cheese combination. The colour and fragrance are those of summer fruits and the Cabernet Sauvignon component gives the warmth of the Mediterranean to the table.

baked salmon with white miso

serves 4

4 salmon fillets, 175 g / 6 oz each,
centre part, with skin (get fishmonger
to cut fillet at an angle rather than
straight cut as it will marinate better
in the miso dressing)

white miso dressing
450 g / 1 lb white miso paste
175 ml / 6 fl oz mirin
250 g / 9 oz granulated sugar

wasabi-parsnip purée
3 medium size parsnips,
peeled, cut into pieces
1 teaspoon wasabi paste
1 tablespoon crème fraiche
salt and pepper
1 tablespoon cream (optional)

baby leaf salad or mixed
sprouts salad
4 teaspoons beni shoga (optional)

White miso dressing
In a sauce pot, combine miso paste and mirin together on low heat.

Use wooden spoon to stir until miso paste has dissolved fully. Add sugar and turn the heat to medium high, stirring constantly until it just comes to boiling point. Make sure the bottom of the pot does not burn.

Take the pot off the heat and allow to cool to room temperature.

Wasabi-parsnip purée
Cook parsnips in lightly salted water until they become soft. Drain and place in a food processor with wasabi paste and crème fraiche and blend until smooth.

Season to taste with salt and pepper. For a lighter purée, add cream.

Salmon
Pat dry the salmon fillets with paper towels. Place the fish in a flat deep dish, cover with white miso dressing and cover tightly with cling film. Make sure the white miso dressing covers all the fillets. Refrigerate for 2 to 3 days.

Take the salmon out of the refrigerator and wipe off any excess white miso dressing.

Do not rinse the fish. Place the fish skin side up on a non-stick baking sheet or on baking parchment paper. Place in oven and bake for about 15 minutes.

To serve, arrange the salmon on each plate. Place the wasabi-parsnip purée on the side and baby leaf salad on top. Garnish with beni shoga (if using).

Notes
Miso is a Japanese soybean paste, popular in soups and many other dishes.
Mirin is a seasoning cooking wine.
Wasabi is hot green horseradish used for sushi and many other dishes.
Beni shoga is a Japanese red-colour pickle of ginger strips.

Champagne is the best accompaniment for sushi; however, as with most Asian dishes,
an Alsace Riesling works well too.

salmon baked in parchment

serves 4

4 salmon fillets, 175 g / 6 oz each,
skinned
2 carrots, cut into fine sticks
2 celery stalks, cut into fine sticks
50 g / 2 oz butter
salt and black pepper

Preheat the oven to 200 °C / 400 °F / Gas mark 6.
Cut out 8 circles of greaseproof paper, 20–25 cm / 8–10 inches in diameter, and grease
with butter. Place four of the circles on a large baking sheet and divide the vegetables
equally between them.
Place a salmon fillet on top of the vegetables and put some butter, salt and pepper on
top of the salmon. Cover with the other circles of greased parchment and roll the edges
tightly together to ensure steam and juices are kept in. Bake for 20 minutes.
Serve immediately, placing one parchment on each of four heated plates, slitting
the centre of the paper at the table, allowing the aroma to escape and the juices
to flow – and causing a bit of a stir and a conversation piece!

Baked potatoes or potato rösti make a good accompaniment for this dish (see p. 135).

Chardonnay, Pouilly-Fuissé, 'Terres du Menhir', Burgundy, France. This dish requires a wine of
style and elegance, and this one will deliver. On the nose there are hints of white flower and stone
fruit. Preferably, choose a wine 3–4 years old.

wild Moy salmon, Clew Bay brown crab ravioli, garden peas, lovage beurre blanc

serves 8

8 wild Moy salmon darnes,
175 g / 6 oz each, with skin, scaled
(see p. 10) and pin-boned
25 ml / 1 fl oz rapeseed oil
sea salt and ground white pepper
nasturtium flowers and lemon
balm shoots to garnish

ravioli pasta
225 g / 8 oz '00' pasta flour
3 eggs
1 egg, lightly beaten, for wash
1 pinch saffron strands
25 ml / 1 fl oz olive oil
110 ml / 4 fl oz water

ravioli filling
450 g / 1 lb brown crab meat
pinch cayenne pepper
pepper
salt

lovage beurre blanc
110 ml / 4 fl oz white wine
1 lemon, juice
2 shallots, diced
pinch thyme
1 bay leaf
200 g / 7 oz cold butter, diced
25 g / 1 oz lovage, chopped

garden peas
1 kg / 2 lb 4 oz garden peas,
in pod
2 litres / 3½ pints water
200 g / 7 oz salt

Ravioli pasta
Combine the flour, saffron, eggs and olive oil in a bowl until the mixture resembles breadcrumbs. Knead to form a dough, wrap in cling film and leave to rest for 30 minutes in the refrigerator. Remove dough from refrigerator and allow it come up to room temperature before rolling. This is important, as it allows the gluten to relax, making the dough more flexible and easier to work with.

Roll the pasta dough through a pasta machine, starting from the widest setting and gradually going down the settings until the arrow is between 0 and 1. Repeat the rolling process on the last setting to ensure there is a consistent thickness to the dough. The pasta should be dry, but with no cracks, and slightly elastic.

Ravioli filling
Mix crab meat and cayenne pepper, add seasoning to taste. Refrigerate until ready to use.

Ravioli assembly
Cut the sheets of rolled pasta into 50 cm / 20 inch lengths. Place a sheet of pasta on a lightly floured work surface and brush lightly with the egg wash. Place small teaspoons of the crab mixture on the sheet, with 10 cm / 4 inch gaps between, in two rows. There should be 8 balls of crab in total on the sheet of pasta. Take another sheet of pasta and gently cover the crab balls that have been placed on the base sheet. Stretch the dough over to meet the edges of the bottom pasta sheet and press gently around each crab ball to form a dome. Using an 8 cm / 3 inch pastry cutter, cut out the ravioli around the crab balls. Pick each of the ravioli up individually and, using your thumb and forefinger, squeeze out any air and seal the edges. Store on a tray lined with a clean tea towel. Repeat the process until all of the crab mix is enclosed.

Lovage beurre blanc
Put the diced shallot, white wine, lemon juice, thyme and bay leaf into a saucepan and simmer slowly until the liquid reduces by half (see p. 12). Add the diced cold butter very slowly and whisk to make an emulsion. Once the emulsion is complete, do not allow the sauce to boil or it will split.
Pass the sauce through a fine sieve and keep the sauce in a small pan at a very low temperature.
At the last minute, just before you serve the sauce, add the fresh lovage.

Garden peas
Remove the fresh peas from their pods. Bring water with salt to the boil, cook the peas for about 30 seconds, strain, and refresh them in ice-cold water. The salt in the boiling water and the refreshing in iced water will keep the colour of the peas fresh. They can be reheated just before serving.

Darnes
Heat a non-stick pan and add rapeseed oil. Season the salmon darnes with sea salt and ground white pepper. Cook the salmon skin side down slowly for about 5 minutes, turn over and cook for 2 more minutes maximum. Stop cooking the fish when the protein of the fish starts to coagulate – little white dots form on the side of the fish. Remove the skin and the fat (brown flesh on the surface of the fish) from the salmon.

Finishing and serving
Cook the ravioli in salted boiling water for 2–3 minutes, until the pasta is just cooked.
Reheat the garden peas with a knob of butter.

Serve the salmon with the crab ravioli on top and peas around it. Pour the sauce slowly on top and garnish the dish with a nasturtium flower and few lemon balm shoots.

Sancerrre, Bouchard Aîné & Fils, 2010. A sophisticated and elegant dry wine. This has the classic character of fine Sancerre: very fresh, dry, and a crisp lemon flavour.

Executive Chef **Martijn Kajuiter** ❀ ONE MICHELIN STAR *The House Restaurant, The Cliff House Hotel* *Ardmore, Co. Waterford*

EURO-TOQUES theclilffhousehotel.com

Bantry Bay salmon, poached, cured, marinated, iced, oak-smoked, with beetroot preparations and horseradish

My version of smoked salmon was introduced on 19 May 2008 and has evolved over the years to where it is today. The instant smoke idea was fairly new in the gastronomic landscape at that time. It is one of those dishes which will remain on the menu forever.

serves 8–10

ballotine of salmon
whole side of organic salmon,
pin-boned, with skin
½ lemon, zest
pinch fine sea salt
black pepper, freshly ground

cured salmon
1 lemon, fine zest
1 orange, fine zest
50 ml / 2 fl oz Cork Dry Gin
50 g / 2 oz parsley
50 g / 2 oz dill
50 g / 2 oz chervil
50 g / 2 oz chives
50 ml / 2 fl oz beetroot juice
75 g / 3 oz coarse sea salt
25 g / 1 oz sugar
black pepper, freshly ground

salmon ice cream
300 ml / ½ pint low-fat milk
225 g / 8 oz smoked salmon
15 g / ½ oz grated horseradish
20 g / ¾ oz glycerine
25 g / 1 oz glucose
20 g / ¾ oz dextrose
seasoning

beetroot
2 yellow beetroots
3 red beetroots
fennel leaf
1 teaspoon olive oil
1 teaspoon lemon, zest
110 ml / 4 fl oz orange juice
seasoning
1 Chioggia beet and 1 yellow
beetroot, for shaving

Ballotine of salmon
Using a sharp knife, cut the belly away from the back of the salmon, being careful not to cut through the skin and leaving the skin on the salmon back. Scrape any remaining flesh and bloodline off the skin and cut off the tail end. Season the salmon back with salt, pepper and lemon zest. Wrap the skin around it.

Spread cling film on the work surface, place salmon back in the middle and roll to a tight sausage. Leave to set overnight. Next day, remove the cling film.
Poach the salmon at 42 °C / 108 °F for 34 minutes. Cool directly and let it set in the fridge.

Cured salmon belly
Place the herbs on a drying rack overnight. When dry, blitz into powder and sieve until extra-fine dust. Rub the salmon belly all over with the sea salt. Sprinkle with sugar, ground pepper and zest of lemon and orange. Place in vacuum bag and add the Cork Dry Gin.
Vacuum at full programme and leave to cure for a minimum of 36 hours in the fridge.
After the cure time, remove belly from vacuum pack and divide in two equal pieces.
Re-pack one half with the beetroot juice and infuse for a further 24 hours.
The other half is kept plain and coated with the herb dust.

Ice cream
Combine all ingredients and blend into a smooth mixture. Place in a plastic container and freeze.

Beetroot reduction
Put beetroot juice, oil and gelatine in a pot and simmer on low heat until reduced (see p. 12) by a third. Sieve and set aside.

Beetroot
Cook the red beetroots in a pot of water until soft. Peel 1 beetroot and slice in a desired shape, marinate with olive oil, fennel leaf and seasoning. Purée the other 2 beetroots with olive oil and lemon juice until silky. Add seasoning.
Peel the yellow beetroots. Using a pearler, scoop out very small balls. Cook the pearls in the orange juice until tender but with a bite. Season to taste.
Dice the leftover bits of raw yellow beetroot, cook in boiling salted water until soft and purée.
Peel the Chioggia and the other yellow beetroot for shaving later.

Cucumber
With the smallest pearler, scoop out small cucumber balls. Place in a small Kilner jar and add the vinegar, sugar, tarragon and salt. Marinate for a minimum of 2 hours.

Photography Martin Morell

horseradish and lemon mayonnaise

250 ml / 9 fl oz groundnut oil
1 egg yolk
1½ teaspoons mustard
½ teaspoon Worcester sauce
15 g / ½ oz horseradish, freshly grated
2 teaspoons lemon juice
1 lemon, zest
salt and pepper

cucumber pearls

¼ cucumber
25 ml / 1 fl oz cider vinegar
1 teaspoon sugar
2 sprigs tarragon
salt

beetroot reduction

150 ml / 5 fl oz beetroot juice
2 teaspoons olive oil
½ sheet gelatine

garnish

salmon roe
oyster leaf
borage flower
beetroot leaf

Horseradish and lemon mayonnaise

Put the egg yolk, mustard, Worcester sauce, lemon juice and seasoning in a mixing bowl. Whisk until smooth. Drop by drop, whisk in the oil until a smooth thick mixture is achieved. Add the grated horseradish and lemon zest. Preserve in the fridge until use.

Presentation

Slice the ballotine in 2 cm / ¾ inch pieces. Set a slice in the middle of each plate, with a tranche of both beetroot-cured and herb-coated salmon belly beside it.

Arrange small dots of the beetroot purées, beetroot reduction and mayonnaise on the plate.

Then arrange the sliced and pearled cucumber, the cucumber pearls and the salmon roe on the plate.

Decorate the dish playfully with the flowers, leaves and beetroot shavings (use a mandolin to shave thin slices of the beetroot). Finish with a scoop of salmon ice cream.

Cover the plate with a glass dome and, immediately before serving, blow oak smoke under it to flavour the dish. A maximum of 45 seconds is advised between smoking and releasing the smoke to prevent over-smoking.

Viognier, Petit Manseng, Chardonnay, Chenin Blanc, Mas de Daumas Gassac, Languedoc, France. A fine alternative to more expensive Burgundy whites. This is the wine of first choice of the Languedoc. It is complex in structure, as can be expected with the variety of grapes. White stone fruits and minerality give balance and depth.

salmon fillet with braised cabbage and smoked rasher

This recipe is very suitable for a St Patrick's Day celebration, combining quintessential Irish ingredients in a modern take.

serves 4

4 salmon fillets, 175 g / 6 oz each, skin left on
6 smoked rashers, chopped
3 cloves garlic, finely chopped
½ head green cabbage, chopped in ribbons
50 g / 2 oz butter
2 tablespoons capers
4 sprigs of dill, chopped
juice of 1 lemon
sunflower oil, for frying
knob of butter, for frying
pinch of salt and pepper

Preheat oven to 150 °C / 300 °F / Gas mark 2.

Heat a heavy-based frying pan until very hot.

Add the sunflower oil and butter and fry the salmon, skin side down, for 3 minutes.

Turn and cook other side for 2–3 minutes until golden. Remove salmon and keep warm in oven.

Heat pan, add sunflower oil and fry chopped rashers until crisp.

Remove rashers, add cabbage and garlic and fry gently for about 5 minutes.

Add three-quarters of rasher bits to cabbage mix and keep warm.

Melt butter in a small saucepan, add capers, dill and lemon juice, and heat through.

Place cabbage mix on heated plates, arrange salmon on top and drizzle with melted butter mixture. Garnish with remaining crispy rasher.

Creamy mashed potatoes go well with this. For a creamy mash, use crème fraiche or light cream cheese in the mash.

Sauvignon Blanc, Lawson's Dry Hills, Marlborough, New Zealand. This rich aromatic bouquet will mix well with the strong flavours here. The passionfruit, gooseberry and melon flavours are delicious.

Sláinte an bhradáin dhuit
The health of the salmon to you

conservation of wild salmon

We may imagine that the seas are heaving with Atlantic salmon, but in essence there are now only around three million salmon in the whole of the North Atlantic at any one time. Even when salmon were at peak abundance in the 1960s, there were probably no more than 10 million fish at sea, to be shared between the continents of North America and Europe.

For the past two decades scientists have become increasingly concerned that survival has plummeted for some stocks of Atlantic salmon. The cause of this worrying phenomenon lies in the oceans, which are changing not just in terms of surface temperature but also biologically. The distribution of the shrimp-like creatures which form the plankton communities in the surface layers of our neighbouring seas is altering at a significant rate.

Species adapted to the colder waters in which salmon smolts thrive are moving north, and new, exotic forms from the south now inhabit those vacated ecological niches. We also now know that is it is not simply the quantity of food available to the feeding salmon that is important but also the array of organisms and the quality of the nutrition they provide. Movement north by the prey species has profound implications.

Research has shown that the potential impact on the more southerly stocks of salmon, including fish from Spain, France, Ireland and the UK, is greatest and that salmon from more northerly climes, such as Norway and Russia, are faring better.

Worried that over-harvesting of salmon was adding to the plight of the wild salmon, the Irish authorities have in recent years introduced a revolutionary new salmon management system which takes account of each individual stock or population of salmon in the various Irish rivers – over 140 in total. Each autumn the status of the individual stocks is estimated from catch returns and a range of fish counting methods. Estimates are made of the probable returns which can be expected the following year and quotas are struck for both the commercial and the sport fisheries. In this way only salmon which are surplus to the spawning requirements of each river are harvested and the consumer can be sure that any wild salmon on sale in Irish retail outlets is from a fully sustainable wild salmon fishery.

coexistence of wild and farmed salmon

As wild salmon becomes rarer and more expensive, another option for the concerned consumer is to purchase farmed salmon. In Ireland, we began to experiment with salmon farming in the mid-1970s, and by the late 1970s and early 1980s several pilot farms had been established. Farmed stocks in Ireland have thrived, and despite the modest size of the industry it has achieved an important market share, particularly in relation to the quality of the product.

The move to semi-offshore sites has brought with it yet further improvement in quality, and many in the industry are of the view that the future of the Irish farmed salmon lies in the quality niche area rather than in attempting to compete with the giant producers such as Norway and Scotland.

The west coast of Ireland is a good deal more exposed than the sheltered fjords of Norway and the sheltered bays of the west coast of Scotland. As a result, the fledgling Irish industry experienced great difficulty in terms of cage design: the enclosures needed to be strong enough to withstand the force of mid-winter Atlantic gales. Such physical limitations constrained the expansion of the Irish industry, along with issues relating to licensing of sites.

A major factor in stalling the growth of the industry was the bitter controversy of the late 1980s and early 1990s, which developed along the west coast in relation to the impact of the fledgling farming industry on Irish sea-trout stocks. Within a few short years the devastating impact of sea lice from poorly managed farms on neighbouring wild sea-trout stocks was clear, and there was incontrovertible scientific evidence linking lice levels on farms with the loss of major sea-trout stocks. Management methods developed and established throughout the 1980s and 1990s, including single-bay management and separation of year classes, have the potential to ensure that the salmon farming industry can coexist in areas where wild salmonids are present.

The coexistence of the two industries is totally dependent on an understanding and an appreciation of the requirements of the wild salmonids. In a wider context, the salmon farming industry must learn to live within the biological constraints of the selected fish farming bays and to exist in harmony with the myriad wild creatures living in these bays, while at the same time providing a modest home for concentrations of farmed fish.

Research on growing salmon in closed-containment recirculation systems has also shown encouraging results, and it is hoped that a fine balance between the farmed salmon and recreational angling industries can be found in the very near future. **KW**

accompaniments

shortcrust pastry case for flan

225 g / 8 oz plain flour
110 g / 4 oz butter, cold and cubed
1 egg yolk
2–3 tablespoons water, chilled
pinch salt

Sieve the flour and salt into a bowl.
Rub in the butter until you have a soft breadcrumb texture.
Add the beaten egg yolk and enough water to combine the mix.
Gently knead the pastry, wrap in cling film and rest in the fridge for 30 minutes.
Preheat the oven to 190 °C / 375 °F/ Gas mark 5.
Butter a 20 cm / 8 inch flan tin.
Roll out the pastry on a lightly floured board and roll until wide enough to cover the flan tin.
Carefully place pastry in flan tin, prick the base with a fork, and rest and chill again for about 15 minutes.
Remove the tin from the fridge, line the pastry case with baking parchment and fill with baking or dried beans. Place the tin on a hot baking sheet and bake for 20 minutes. This is called blind baking.
After 20 minutes remove the beans and paper and return the pastry to the oven for another 2–3 minutes.
Remove the tin from the oven, leave to cool. Leave the pastry in the tin, and this flan case is ready for the filling of your choice.

Melba toast

Melba toast is a dry, crisp and thinly sliced toast that makes a wonderful base for a pâté or mousse. The name is thought to date to 1897, when renowned chef Auguste Escoffier reputedly created this toast for Dame Nellie Melba when the Australian opera singer was very ill and resident in the Savoy Hotel in London, where Escoffier was head chef. He also created Peach Melba in her honour.

2 slices day-old white sliced pan

Preheat the grill to its highest setting.
Toast the bread until pale golden-brown on both sides.
When the toast is cool enough to handle, remove crusts. Using a sharp knife, carefully cut each slice in half through the soft centre to form four thinner slices.
Place the toast slices, uncooked sides facing upwards, under the grill again and toast until pale golden-brown.
Reduce the heat of the grill to its lowest setting.
Cut each slice of Melba toast into triangles and grill for a further few seconds on each side until crisp and golden-brown on all sides.

hollandaise sauce

Hollandaise sauce is a classic butter sauce. It is an emulsion of egg yolk and butter, usually seasoned with lemon juice, salt and a little white pepper or cayenne pepper.

3 egg yolks
1 tablespoon water
1 tablespoon fresh lemon juice,
200 g / 7 oz unsalted butter, softened and cubed
cayenne pepper
salt
freshly ground white pepper

Put the water, vinegar and lemon juice in a small bowl, add the egg yolks and, using a balloon whisk, whisk until pale and frothy.
Place the bowl over a pan of simmering water and continue to whisk at reasonable speed until the mixture thickens. Cube by cube, add the soft butter, whisking constantly until fully absorbed. Continue incorporating butter until the sauce has thickened to the consistency you want. If it looks like it might split, remove from the heat and continue to whisk. Season lightly with salt, white pepper and a dash of cayenne pepper, whisking in well.
Serve lukewarm.

horseradish cream

300 ml / ½ pint double cream
1 tablespoon fresh horseradish, peeled and grated
1 tablespoon horseradish relish
1 tablespoon Dijon mustard
1 lemon, juiced
8 sprigs chervil

Put all the ingredients in a blender and mix until slightly thick.
Cover and store in the refrigerator until needed.

quick mayonnaise

2 egg yolks
300 ml / ½ pint olive oil
1 lemon, juice
salt and white pepper

Put the egg yolks and salt in a blender and blend slowly.
While motor is running, very slowly pour in the oil until you get a thick and smooth consistency.
Add the lemon juice and taste for seasoning.

Caesar salad dressing

1 garlic clove, roughly chopped
2 anchovy fillets, roughly chopped
3 tablespoons mayonnaise (see left)
1 tablespoon olive oil
½ lemon juice
3 tablespoons grated parmesan
1 bunch spring onions, finely chopped

Using a mortar and pestle, pound the garlic and anchovy fillets to a paste. Mix with the mayonnaise, olive oil, lemon juice and Parmesan. Season to taste.

Marie Rose or cocktail sauce

This sauce is an icon of the 1970s. The sauce, and the prawn cocktail with which it is most commonly associated, was created by renowned British cook Fanny Cradock in the 1960s.

4 tablespoons mayonnaise (see p. 134)
1½ tablespoons tomato ketchup
dash Tabasco sauce
dash Worcestershire sauce
1 tablespoon lemon juice
dash brandy (optional)

Place all of the ingredients together in a bowl and mix until well combined. Taste and add more lemon, Tabasco or Worcestershire sauce as desired.

watercress sauce

225 g / 8 oz watercress leaves
3 cloves garlic, crushed
2 tablespoons fresh tarragon, chopped
275 g / 10 oz mayonnaise (see p. 134)
2 tablespoons lemon juice
200 g / 7 oz unsalted butter, melted

Using a blender, put the watercress, mayonnaise, garlic, tarragon and lemon juice in a bowl and blend until well mixed.
While continuing to blend, very slowly pour in the melted butter, little by little, until you get a nice thick and smooth consistency.
Cover and chill before serving.

hazelnut pesto

25 g /1 oz toasted hazelnuts, chopped
handful of basil leaves
1 clove garlic, chopped
3 tablespoons extra-virgin olive oil
1 tablespoon Parmesan cheese, freshly grated
sea salt and pepper

Place all the ingredients in a blender and blend until smooth.

Sautéed ribbons of courgettes tossed in this pesto are so tasty and go really well with salmon.

lemon butter sauce

The rich silky texture of this sauce makes it a perfect accompaniment for salmon. This is not a sauce that can be made in advance and reheated, but its melting buttery flavour will reward the effort nonetheless.

2 tablespoons white wine
juice of 1 lemon
finely grated zest of ½ lemon
1 tablespoon double cream
225 g / 8 oz unsalted butter, chilled and cubed
sea salt and freshly ground white pepper

Boil the white wine, lemon juice and zest for 1 minute.
Stir in the cream, add the butter and whisk briskly until the butter is amalgamated and the sauce slightly thickened.
Season with the salt and pepper.
Serve immediately.

béchamel sauce

300 ml / ½ pint milk
1 medium onion, peeled
1 bay leaf
5–6 white peppercorns
25 g / 1 oz butter
25 g /1 oz plain flour
pinch salt

Pour the milk into a saucepan, add the onion, bay leaf and peppercorns and simmer over a very low heat for 5–10 minutes until the flavours infuse.
Strain the milk into a jug discarding the peppercorns, onion and bay leaf.
Put the milk and the remaining ingredients into a saucepan, place over a medium heat.
Using a balloon whisk, continue whisking until the sauce is cooked and thickened.

dulse muffins

Dulse or dillisk, or creathnach as I knew it, is easily found on our shores. It has a high protein content and is a good source of minerals and vitamins, as well as all the trace elements needed by humans. What's not to like?

225 g / 8 oz white self-raising flour
1 teaspoon dulse, finely chopped
1 medium egg, beaten
3 tablespoons sunflower oil
150 ml / ¼ pint milk

Preheat the oven to 190 °C / 375 °F / Gas mark 5. Grease six muffin tins. Mix the flour and dulse together in a bowl. Mix the beaten egg with the oil and a few tablespoons of the milk. Make a well in the centre of the flour, pour in the egg mixture and mix from the centre out with a wooden spoon. Add enough of the remaining milk to make a very soft dough. Spoon the mixture into greased muffin tins and bake in the centre of the oven for 15–20 minutes. Remove from the tins and cool on a wire rack.

potato rösti

450 g / 1 lb floury potatoes (such as Rooster or Kerr's Pink)
salt and pepper
rapeseed oil, for frying

Peel the potatoes and coarsely grate on to a clean tea towel.
After you have grated 2 potatoes, roll the tea towel and twist the ends to squeeze out as much moisture as possible.
Repeat until all potatoes are grated, season with a teaspoon of salt and some grated pepper.
Heat some oil in a 25 cm / 10 inch frying pan.
Add the potato mix and press down evenly to cover the base of the pan.
Fry over a low to medium heat for about 12–15 minutes until golden-brown underneath.
Using a spatula, flip it over and cook the other side for the same length of time until golden.
Check in between that you have sufficient oil on the pan, and add a little more if needed. Serve warm.

tomato concassé

Concassé is simply a term for a mixture that is coarsely chopped or puréed. Tomato is one of the most common ingredients used in concassé. If you use concasséed tomatoes when cooking, the dish will be less watery than if you use whole tomatoes.

4 tomatoes
water, for boiling
iced water, for cooling

With a paring knife, score the tomatoes with an X at the opposite end to the stem. Immerse the tomatoes in boiling water for 10 seconds or until they start to blister. Plunge them into iced water immediately until cold. Peel off the skin and cut in half cross-ways. Hold the tomato halves cut side down and squeeze to rid them of their seeds and water, or scoop them out with your finger. Dice the seedless peeled tomatoes and refrigerate for later use.

coriander-flavoured oil

large bunch coriander
110 ml / 4 fl oz extra-virgin
olive oil

Blanch the coriander leaves for 30 seconds in boiling water or until the leaves turn bright green. Using a tongs or a sieve, remove coriander from water and plunge into very cold water to stop cooking process. Drain well, put into a jar, add olive oil and mix. Cover and keep refrigerated until needed.

hazelnut dressing

3 tablespoons hazelnuts roasted, skinned, and finely chopped
4 tablespoons extra-virgin olive oil
1 tablespoon white wine vinegar
½ tablespoon Dijon mustard
pinch caster sugar
salt and freshly ground white pepper

Place all the ingredients, except the hazelnuts, in a screw-topped jar. Shake the contents well until you have a nice thick emulsion. Season with salt and pepper. Add the hazelnuts. Chill until needed.

Alan Fitmaurice's rye bread

2 loaves

400 g / 14 oz rye flour
400 g / 14 oz wholemeal spelt flour
110 g / 4 oz strong white flour
2 teaspoons easy-bake dried yeast
1 teaspoon fine sea salt
600 ml / 1 pint warm water
3 tablespoons honey

Put the flours into a warm, large mixing bowl with the dried yeast and salt, and mix well.

Lightly warm the water and add the honey, stirring to dissolve, then pour into the flour and yeast. Mix the ingredients to form a dough, then tip on to a floured board or work surface.

Form the dough into a ball, and knead by hand for 4 or 5 minutes.

Lightly oil the bowl then return the dough to it, cover with a tea cloth or cling film, then set aside in a warm place for about an hour, until the dough has doubled in size.

Preheat the oven to 220 °C / 425 °F / Gas mark 7.

Dust two 900 g / 2 lb loaf tins with flour.

Remove the dough from the bowl, place on a lightly floured board and knead again, briefly, for just a minute or two.

Divide the dough in half, then place in the prepared loaf tins, cover and set aside for a further 30 minutes until risen.

Bake for 30 minutes, until crisp on top.

Remove from the oven, leave for 10 minutes in its tin, then lift out and leave to cool before slicing.

Kevin Thornton's fish stock

250 g / 9 oz fish bones, e.g. whiting, sole or turbot (avoid oily fish such as mackerel, salmon, red mullet)
3 leeks
1 fennel bulb
3 shallots
1 bouquet garni (celery heart, thyme sprig, flat-leaf parsley sprig, bay leaf, all tied together)
175 ml / 6 fl oz white wine
1 litre / 1¾ pints cold still water
1 teaspoon whole white peppercorns

Rinse the fish bones and trimmings of any blood, otherwise this will make the stock look cloudy and taste bitter. Chop the leeks roughly and place in a large heavy-bottomed stockpot.

Roughly chop the fennel and shallots and add to the stockpot.
Add the white peppercorns and bouquet garni, then add the fish trimmings to the stockpot.

Pour in the white wine and add enough of the water to cover the fish and vegetables. Place the stockpot on a high heat and bring the liquid to a simmer. After 5 minutes, remove the scum that forms on the surface with a spoon and discard. Reduce the heat and simmer, covered, for about 25 minutes, skimming as necessary.

At the end of the cooking time, remove the stock from the heat and strain, discarding the fish trimmings and the vegetables.

Cool and store in the fridge for up to three days or freeze. Alternatively, you can reduce the stock further and then freeze it in ice-cube trays (freezing it this way means you can defrost as little or as much as you need at a time).

Brown bread and smoked salmon is a classic that deserves tasty home-made brown bread. These two recipes were baked every day by two women who prided themselves on the quality of their bread.

Kathleen Ruddy (1914-2004) from Connemara, winner of the 1992 Bog Week Brown Bread Award, and Kathleen Murphy (1922-2013) from Cork, a winner every day for her family, baked fabulous brown bread. We are happy to remember them in this book.

Kathleen Ruddy's brown bread

700 g / 1½ lb plain flour
110 g / 4 oz wheat bran
110 g / 4 oz margarine, melted
1 heaped teaspoon bread soda
1 heaped teaspoon salt
3–4 teaspoons sugar
800 ml / 1½ pints buttermilk

Preheat the oven to 200 °C / 400 °F / Gas mark 6.
Sieve flour and bread soda into a large bowl, add wheat bran, salt and sugar and mix.
Melt the margarine in a small saucepan over low heat. Add half the buttermilk and melted margarine. I like to use a strong knife to mix but a spoon is ok too.
Keep adding buttermilk until it forms a nice dough, then knead by hand. Spread the dough on flour-covered surface. Knead and shape into a circle. Cut in two. Place the two halves on a hot baking tray in oven and bake for 40–45 minutes.
To know when it is cooked, simply tap the bottom of the loaf. It will sound hollow when fully cooked. Wrap in a clean tea towel while cooling. This will keep the crust nice and soft.

Kathleen Murphy's brown bread

110 g / 4 oz white self-raising flour
350 g / 12 oz wholemeal self-raising flour
75 g / 3 oz wheat germ
110 g / 4 oz margarine
pinch salt
300 ml / ½ pint buttermilk

Preheat the oven to 200 °C / 400 °F / Gas mark 6.
Put flour and bread soda into large bowl, add wheat bran, salt and sugar and mix. Rub in the margarine, do not over-handle. Add half the buttermilk and mix in with your fingers, making sure to take off any finger jewellery! Add remaining buttermilk until it forms a nice wet dough, then knead out by hand. Grease a turkey-sized roasting tin. Transfer dough to the tin and 'knuckle' it into shape, leaving room at the sides for a little expansion. With a knife, mark a cross on the dough so you can break it easily into four sections when baked. It also helps the mid-section to cook more evenly. Bake in preheated oven for 50–55 minutes, until golden brown. Remove from the roasting tin using a spatula, and place on a wire rack. Rub the top with a little butter. Cover loosely with a tea towel. For a smaller cake, halve the ingredients.

index of contributors

First published in Ireland 2013
by Artisan House Editions
Letterfrack, Connemara, Co. Galway, Ireland
www.artisanhouse.ie

Editorial Director **Mary Ruddy**

Creative Director **Vincent Murphy**

Author **Máirín Uí Chomáin**
www.irishcuisine.ie

Photographer **Walter Pfeiffer**
www.walterpfeifferstudios.com

Foreword **Ken Whelan**
www.kenwhelan.info

Copy-editor **Rachel McNicholl**
www.afepi.ie/mcnicholl-rachel/

Proof-reader **Joanna McMinn**

Food stylist **Tricia Doyle**
www.triciadoyle.com

Beverage notes **Betty Murphy**

Peter Dunne
www.mitchellandson.com

Printing **KPS Colour Print,** Co. Mayo
www.kpscolourprint.com

Artisan House Editions © 2013
Recipes and text by Máirín Uí Chomáin © Máirín Uí Chomáin 2013
Foreword and contextual text © Ken Whelan 2013
Photography and styling of Máirín's recipes © Walter Pfeiffer 2013

Copyright in the work of contributing chefs and photographers rests with
the individual contributors. The contributors assert their moral right to be
identified as the authors of their work.

All rights reserved.
No part of this publication covered by the copyright may be reproduced
or used in any form or by any means, graphic, electronic or mechanical
including photocopying, recording, taping, web distribution or information
storage retrieval systems without the prior written permission of the
publisher, except for as expressly permitted by law.

ISBN 978-0-9926908-0-9

British Library cataloguing in Publication Data.
A CIP catalogue record for this book is available from the British Library.

PUBLISHER'S ACKNOWLEDGEMENTS

Artisan House gratefully acknowledges the support of Forum Connemara Ltd.
It is very much appreciated.

In developing *Celebrating Irish Salmon*, we called on friends, family and
contributors to perform challenging tasks to demanding standards within
very tight timeframes. And they did.

In particular, we wish to convey our gratitude to Máirín Uí Chomáin, whose
enthusiasm for this book and its subject never waned, and to all the contributing
chefs, food writers, smokehouse producers and individuals who so generously
gave their recipes to made this book as bountiful as it is.

We are very grateful to Ken Whelan, whose expertise and knowledge of the
Atlantic salmon was matched by his helpful insight and suggestions.

The overall visual quality of the book could not have been delivered without
our wonderful photographer friend, Walter Pfeiffer. We thank food stylist
Tricia Doyle for her imaginative presentation of dishes and her advice.
Eagle-eyed copy-editor Rachel McNicholl worked far beyond the original
brief to ensure accuracy and standards throughout the text. Thank you,
Rachel. We are also grateful to our additional proof-reader, Joanna McMinn,
who read the proofs in far Somaliland.

Many thanks to our knowledgeable beverage contributors, Betty Murphy
and Peter Dunne, with whom we had fun sampling quite a few of the pairings.
Thanks to Brendan Salmon and the print production team at KPS Colour
Print in Co. Mayo. Also to all who gave us images to reproduce, in particular
Markus Müller from Fisheries Ireland, photographers James Sadler and
David Lambroughton, and illustrators Ray Murphy and Robin Ade.

We thank the food writers and enthusiasts who commended the book:
Darina Allen, Georgina Campbell, Gillian Nelis and Ernie Whalley.
We are grateful to Mary Kennedy and Georgina Campbell for their
gracious acceptance of our invitations to launch *Celebrating Irish Salmon*
in, respectively, Dublin and Connemara.

Thanks to Caroline Herriott of Cuán Mara Design, who worked tirelessly to
get a magnificent website online; to Debbie Ruddy for her social media and
negotiation skills; to Philip Gooding, who creates spreadsheets like works
of art; to Paddy Ruddy, who worked miracles to make a space for us to work in;
to Grainne O'Malley for her practical support; to Toni Wall, Carley Donegan
and Mikaela Kenny at Wall2Wall PR for their expertise and dedication; to Ruth
Hegarty at Euro-Toques for her invaluable assistance; to John Manning at Gill
& Macmillan for his support; and to Nollaig and Siobhain Ruddy, our dog
Cleo's surrogate walkers. Finally, we thank Laillí Lamb de Buitléar for kind
permission to reproduce the painting *Teach an Droichid, Abhainn Chasla* by
her father, Charles Lamb, RHA.

Mary Ruddy and Vincent Murphy
ARTISAN HOUSE

This project is supported by The European Agricultural Fund for Rural Development – Europe investing in rural areas.